W9-BFD-774

AROUND new york city WITH KIDS

by Mindy Bailin

Fodor's Travel Publications
New York • Toronto • London • Sydney • Auckland

www.fodors.com

CREDITS
Writer: Mindy Bailin

Series Editors: Karen Cure, Caroline Haberfeld
Editor: Andrea Lehman
Editorial Production: Nicole Revere
Production/Manufacturing: Robert Shields

Design: Fabrizio La Rocca, *creative director*;
Tigist Getachew, *art director*
Illustration and Series Design: Rico Lins, Keren Ora
Admoni/Rico Lins Studio

ABOUT THE WRITER

New York resident Mindy Bailin is a teacher and mother of three who writes frequently about health, family, and education for many newspapers and magazines.

First Edition
ISBN 0–679–00490–4
ISSN 1526–1468

Important Tip

Although all prices, opening times, and other details in this book are based on information supplied to us at press time, changes occur all the time in the travel world, and Fodor's cannot accept responsibility for facts that become outdated or for inadvertent errors or omissions. So always confirm information when it matters, especially if you're making a detour to visit a specific place.

Special Sales

Fodor's Travel Publications are available at special discounts for bulk purchases for sales promotions or premiums. Special editions, including personalized covers, excerpts of existing guides, and corporate imprints, can be created in large quantities for special needs. For more information, contact your local bookseller or Special Markets, Fodor's Travel Publications, 201 East 50th Street, New York, NY 10022. Inquiries from Canada should be directed to your local Canadian bookseller or sent to Random House of Canada, Ltd., Marketing Dept., 2775 Matheson Boulevard East, Mississauga, Ontario L4W 4P7. Inquiries from the United Kingdom should be sent to Fodor's Travel Publications, 20 Vauxhall Bridge Road, London, England SW1V 2SA.

PRINTED IN THE UNITED STATES OF AMERICA
10 9 8 7 6 5 4 3 2 1

CONTENTS

WELCOME TO GREAT DAYS!

Between pick-ups, drop-offs, and after-school activities, organizing a family's schedule is one full-time job. Planning for some fun time together shouldn't be another. That's where this book helps out. In creating it, our parent-experts have done all the legwork, so you don't have to. Open to any page and you'll find a great day together already planned out. You can read about the main event, check our age-appropriateness ratings to make sure it's right for your family, pick up some smart tips, and find out where to grab a bite nearby.

HOW TO SAVE MONEY
Taking a whole family on an outing can be pricey, but there are ways to save.

1. Always ask about discounts at ticket booths. We list admission prices only for adults and kids, but an affiliation (and your ID) may get you a break. If you want to support a specific institution, consider buying a family membership up front. Usually these pay for themselves after a couple of visits, and sometimes they come with other good perks—gift-shop and parking discounts, and so on.

2. Keep an eye peeled for coupons. They'll save you $2 or $3 a head and you can find them everywhere from the supermarket to your pediatrician's office. Combination tickets, sometimes offered by groups of attractions, cost less than if you pay each admission individually.

3. Try to go on free days. Some attractions let you in at no charge one day a month or one day a week after a certain time.

GOOD TIMING

Most attractions with kid appeal are busy when school is out. Field-trip destinations are sometimes swamped on school days, but these groups tend to leave by early afternoon, so weekdays after 2 during the school year can be an excellent time to visit museums, zoos, and aquariums. Outdoors, consider going after a rain—there's nothing like a downpour to clear away crowds. If you go on a holiday, call ahead—we list only the usual operating hours.

SAFETY CATCH

Take a few sensible precautions. Show your kids how to recognize staff or security people when you arrive. And designate a meeting time and place—some visible landmark—in case you become separated. It goes without saying that you should keep a close eye on your children at all times, especially if they are small.

FINAL THOUGHTS

We'd love to hear yours: What did you and your kids think about the places we recommend? Have you found other places we should include? Send us your ideas via e-mail (c/o editors@fodors.com, specifying the name of this book on the subject line) or snail mail (c/o Around New York City with Kids, Fodor's Travel Publications, 201 East 50th Street, New York, NY 10022). In the meantime, have a great day around New York with your kids!

THE EDITORS

AMERICAN MUSEUM OF THE
MOVING IMAGE

68

L ights! Camera! Action! For any fan of film or television, this museum is *the* place to see the nation's largest and most comprehensive public collection of film and video artifacts. From Thomas Edison's Projecting Kinescope (c. 1897) to computer files used to design film sets in the 1990s, from the earliest existing television receiver (1927) to the most recent video arcade games, the museum has a wealth of materials from motion pictures, TV, and interactive media.

The core exhibition, Behind the Scenes, explores how films and videos are created, how they find their audiences, and how their place in our culture has evolved over the last century. Documenting the production, promotion, and exhibition of motion pictures and television, the exhibit displays such tools of the trade as cameras, microphones, video recorders, and related equipment.

Among the collection of moving-image artifacts are costumes, posters, set-design models, fan magazines, and licensed merchandise such as dolls, lunch boxes, and Flintstone toys. You and

KEEP IN MIND The museum offers a number of programs to enhance your visit. Movie-making exhibits are especially engaging when explained by a tour guide. Free tours are given weekdays at 3; call ahead to reserve space. Also ask about special events, such as guest speakers. Each year an array of famous film and TV actors, directors, and filmmakers make personal appearances at the museum to discuss their craft. Though these are primarily of interest to adults, some will certainly interest kids, especially teenagers. Recent speakers have included cartoonist Chuck Jones and director Spike Lee.

35th Ave. and 36th St., Astoria, Queens

 $8.50 adults, $5.50 youths 13–18, $4.50 children 6–12

 T–F 12–5, Sa–Su 11–6

718/784–4520

7 and up

your children can view the original Yoda puppet from *The Empire Strikes Back,* a collection of Bill Cosby sweaters, Robin Williams's costume from *Mork and Mindy,* and an exact reproduction of the actor as Mrs. Doubtfire. Where else can you see a gold-plated chariot from the 1959 film *Ben Hur* alongside a collection of Fonzie paper dolls?

The museum occupies a 60,000-square-foot building across from the 13-acre Kaufman Astoria Studios complex, where the *Cosby* and *Sesame Street* series are produced. Look for the address the next time Big Bird rolls the credits. Each year in the intimate 200-seat Riklis Theater, more than 300 screenings of television programs and videotapes are presented in their original formats and in the best available prints. Silent films are shown with live musical accompaniment. And don't pass up the neo-Egyptian Tut's Fever Movie Palace, a spoof on a 1920s theater, where hourly movie serials and shorts are screened. Since the films and videos are free, for about the cost of a movie in New York, you can have quite an experience here.

HEY, KIDS! Imagine making your own animated short, dubbing dialogue, or projecting your image onto the costumes of famous stars. Thirteen computer-based activities help explain how a movie is made. You can even see how your dad would look as John Travolta in *Saturday Night Fever!*

KID-FRIENDLY EATS You can catch a light bite in the **museum's café.** Or try the **Christos Hasapo-Taverna** (41-08 23rd Ave., at 41st St., tel. 718/726–5195), a family-friendly restaurant known for quality, service, and value that combines a Greek taverna and steak house. For dessert or a snack, head to Broadway between 31st and 36th streets and follow the aroma of coffee and pastry to an outdoor table at a local pastry shop for baklava or other sweet treats.

AMERICAN MUSEUM OF
NATURAL HISTORY

This museum has been a wonderful place of exploration, discovery, and learning for generations of children. Since it's one of the largest natural history museums in the world, containing over 32 million specimens and cultural artifacts in more than 40 exhibition halls, it's simply not possible to see the entire collection in one visit. The subjects covered range from dinosaurs to gems and minerals, from life in the sea to cultures found around the world to the ends of the cosmos. The wisest course of action is to plan your visit ahead of time (with a narrow focus) and then plan to visit again.

A good place to begin and a must-see on any young visitor's list is the six spectacular halls that house the most comprehensive and scientifically important collection of dinosaurs in the world. Another stop sure to bring a sparkle to your child's eyes is the Hall of Gems, home of the Star of India, the world's largest and most famous blue star sapphire. The Hall of Biodiversity, which opened in 1998, features a multiscreen video projection that gives a global tour of nine ecosystems as well as a 2,500-square-foot diorama that re-creates a

HEY, KIDS!
In 1991, as part of the fossil-halls renovation, the tallest freestanding dinosaur exhibit in the world was erected in the renovated Theodore Roosevelt Memorial Hall. Don't miss this five-story exhibit that features a *Barosaurus* rising up on it back legs to protect its baby from an attacking *Allosaurus*.

KEEP IN MIND
In early 2000, the museum opens the Center for Earth and Space, housing the renovated Hayden Planetarium. A sphere some 90 feet in diameter will contain the most technologically advanced sky theater in the world, as well as the Big Bang Theater, which will present representations of the events that took place during the first moments of the universe. Now that's bang for the buck.

 Central Park West at 79th St.

212/769–5100, 212/769–5200
museum programs and tickets

 Suggested donation $9.50
ages 13 and up, $7.50 students,
$6.50 children 2–12; IMAX extra

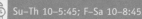 Su–Th 10–5:45; F–Sa 10–8:45

 2 and up

section of an African rain forest. And don't miss the replica of a 94-foot blue whale suspended in the Hall of Ocean Life. Not that you *could* miss it!

If you tire of looking at exhibits, check the IMAX movie schedule for larger-than-life films that reveal nature's wonders, shown daily on a four-story screen. Meanwhile, the Discovery Room welcomes older youngsters and an accompanying adult to explore the scientific process through hands-on exhibits, and the Alexander M. White Natural Science Center gives an introduction to plant and animal life in New York City. But no matter what you think you want to do, call the museum before your visit to get information on current lectures, performances, workshops, and special events for families. There's just so much going on; you'll want to be prepared.

KID-FRIENDLY EATS The **Whale's Lair,** serving snacks Friday–Sunday, and the full-service **Ocean Life Café** are both in the Hall of Ocean Life. The **Diner Saurus** and the **Snack Cart,** in the 77th Street lobby Friday–Sunday, both dispense snacks and sandwiches. For a burger or banana split, try **EJ's Luncheonette** (447 Amsterdam Ave., tel. 212/873–3444).

ASPHALT GREEN

I t has Manhattan's only standard Olympic-size pool, not to mention a separate teaching and exercise pool, a regulation AstroTurf field for sports, two gyms, an indoor and outdoor running track, two outdoor parks, the Mazur Theatre, and indoor and outdoor basketball courts. Whew! Are we finished yet? Not quite. Add to that graphics, photography, and fine arts studios; a duplex fitness center; aerobics rooms; and a physical-therapy/health center. Get the feeling it's worth visiting this campuslike, 5½-acre sports and training complex? Absolutely. And what does "asphalt" have to do with "green," anyway?

Established in 1968 where a former municipal asphalt plant once operated, Asphalt Green was created as a recreational center for city youth and the community at large. The parabolic plant building was declared a New York City landmark and today serves as a full-service sports and fitness complex. The city still owns the land, but in return for rental exemption, Asphalt Green provides a third of its services free to the community.

HEY, KIDS! Meet Olympic swimmers, earn a medal, and get cool free stuff at the annual Big Swim. Top swimmers in each event are invited to participate in an AquaShow, featuring some of the country's best swimmers, lights, music, and a cast of 100 kids. But no matter how good a swimmer you are, if you're ages 6 to 16 you can make a big splash and help raise money for Asphalt Green's Waterproofing program, which teaches thousands of city kids to swim for free.

 555 E. 90th St.

 212/369–8890

 Swim session $15 ages 17 and up, $7 children 16 and under; puppet playhouse $6 ages 2 and up

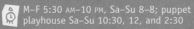 M–F 5:30 AM–10 PM, Sa–Su 8–8; puppet playhouse Sa–Su 10:30, 12, and 2:30

 1 and up, camp kinder-garten–14

As for the "green" portion of its name, the complex also contains Dekovats and Sundial Plaza parks, which feature plenty of green space and gardens, park benches, and game tables. Dekovats adds a playground and a sprinkler during the summer, whereas Sundial Plaza has a fountain.

Children's classes are held in aquatics, sports and fitness, music, and art. Summer camp activities include sports and various arts: of the "fine," "performing," "crafts," and "martial" varieties. February Fun Week and sports minicamps run at different times.

The Lenny Suib Puppet Playhouse at Asphalt Green's Mazur Theatre stages performances with hand puppets, rod puppets, shadow puppets, marionettes, ventriloquists, magicians, storytellers, and clowns as well as exciting guest artists. About the only thing you can't do here anymore is make asphalt.

KID-FRIENDLY EATS A popular food emporium is the **Vinegar Factory** (431 E. 91st St., tel. 212/628–9608). Come for brunch, breakfast, lunch, or dinner for fabulous sandwiches, soups, salads, and pastas. For seafood, barbecued chicken, ribs, and pork, not to mention a kids-eat-free deal, you can't beat **Brother Jimmy's Bait Shack** (1644 3rd Ave., tel. 212/426–2020).

KEEP IN MIND Asphalt Green is available for birthday parties, offering a choice of puppet-show, gymnastics, swimming, or other sports themes as well as a party host. Parties, lasting 1½ hours on weekends only, come with a decorated room, paper goods, and helium balloons. You supply the refreshments, guests, and, of course, the birthday child. No fuss, no mess, no bother.

BROADWAY ON A BUDGET

With tickets for top shows costing up to $80 each, it can be expensive to give your family's regards to Broadway. Enter TKTS. At two locations—at Duffy Square (Times Square) and the World Trade Center—you can purchase discounted tickets to Broadway and Off-Broadway plays and musicals. (Off-Broadway is usually cheaper.) The names of available shows are posted by the booths. You probably won't get tickets to the season's smash hit—after all, they're only made available to TKTS if the theater isn't sold out—but there will undoubtedly be something that's entertaining and/or enlightening.

Each TKTS location has advantages. At the World Trade Center, lines are shorter, you wait indoors, and tickets for matinees and Sundays are sold a day in advance. The wait on the often long line at Duffy Square usually moves fast, however, and if you get your tickets here, you'll be halfway there. You can kill time around Times Square, grab a bite, and walk to the theater. In either spot, though, remember to bring cash or traveler's checks, because TKTS doesn't take American Express—not to mention other credit cards.

KEEP IN MIND Order the free "Family Guide to Broadway" (tel. 212/764–1122 or 800/832–8440) or pick one up at the Convention and Visitor's Bureau (2 Columbus Circle). It contains plots of the season's shows, age guidelines, schedules, prices, running times, and theater locations.

HEY, KIDS! While waiting at Duffy Square, look around at world-famous Times Square! It's where the ball drops on New Year's Eve, the heart of the theater district, and increasingly an exciting hub of wholesome activity. Dazzling billboards contain coffee cups that really steam or 42-foot-high bottles of soda (bet that would quench your thirst!). A superfast ticking digital display shows stock quotes and news, above which are three flashing message boards carrying ads and even a rare marriage proposal.

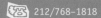 TKTS, Duffy Sq, 47th St. and Broadway;
2 World Trade Center, mezzanine

 Usually 25%–50% off
regular price plus $2.50
surcharge per ticket

 Duffy Sq, M–Sa 3–8, plus W and Sa 10–2,
Su 11–6:30; World Tr Ctr, M–F 11–5:30, Sa 11–3:30

212/768–1818

4 and up, but
varies by show

For the best tickets, get on line early; many people arrive an hour before the booth opens. To avoid a wait, however, go later in the day, but know that many of the day's offerings may be gone. In the fall and nonholiday winter weeks, as many as 50 shows can be available, so don't despair. Family fare can usually be found. Though ticket sellers won't stop and chat about seat locations, the computer automatically lists the "best available" seats. It's likely that your family can sit together, though at the most popular shows, it may be necessary to split into twos and threes.

Another inexpensive way to see well-known long-running shows is to look for bookmark-shape discount coupons, called "twofers." They're distributed by store cash registers, near the TKTS lines, and elsewhere and enable you to buy two tickets for the price of one for selected days and times.

KID-FRIENDLY EATS   Slide into the stadiumlike **Official All Star Cafe** (1540 Broadway, tel. 212/840–8326), which sports a 60-foot ceiling circled by a blimp, 30 giant sports-filled screens, and copious memorabilia. Choose from 17 burger toppings here, or split a gargantuan sandwich at the **Stage Deli** (834 7th Ave., tel. 212/245–7850). Don't forget the pickles. Also *see* NBC Studios Backstage Tour, the New Victory Theater, Radio City Music Hall, and Rockefeller Center and the Ice Rink.

BRONX ZOO

64

Officially called the Bronx Zoo Wildlife Conservation Park, this is the country's largest metropolitan wildlife park, home to more than 6,400 animals, including endangered and threatened species. But the exhibits here aren't fenced areas containing standard zoo animals. One example is the World of Darkness, where your children are suddenly up way past their bedtimes to get a "night view" of such nocturnal animals as leopard cats, cloud rats, and lemurs. They can peek at a subterranean naked mole rat colony or journey to the Himalayan Highlands to spot elusive and endangered snow leopards, fiery red pandas, and white-naped cranes.

The 265-acre zoo is too big to cover in a day and big enough to warrant returning again and again. With young children, begin in the north in parking lot B (the only year-round lot). Walk west to the Butterfly Zone and Monkey House, loop around the elephants, and land at the Children's Zoo, where learning about animals occurs by doing what animals do. Youngsters can climb a giant spider's web, try on a turtle shell, or escape like a lizard down a hollow tree, exploring five theme areas, including the one where they can pet and feed domesticated

HEY, KIDS! For a birds'-eye view of the entire park, take a cool ride on the Skyfari aerial cable car, or go on the Bengali Express (open May–October), an awesome monorail journey through the forests and meadows of Asia ($2 each). Look out for elephants, rhinoceroses, rare sika deer, antelope, and Siberian tigers all roaming in their open, outdoor habitat. In the summer, head to these two attractions first because lines can be long.

Bronx River Pkwy. and
Fordham Rd., Bronx

718/367-1010

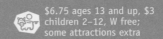
$6.75 ages 13 and up, $3
children 2–12, W free;
some attractions extra

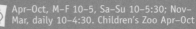
Apr–Oct, M–F 10–5, Sa–Su 10–5:30; Nov–
Mar, daily 10–4:30. Children's Zoo Apr–Oct

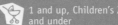
1 and up, Children's Zoo 8
and under

animals. If attention spans hold, walk north to the Aquatic Bird House and the Big Birds (no relation to any Sesame Street neighbors) and east past the bison before leaving.

For older children, begin in Asia Parking A (April–October), to the zoo's south. Walk to Wild Asia to experience JungleWorld, a major indoor exhibit that re-creates an Indonesian scrub forest, mangrove forest, and Southeast Asian rain forest with about 780 animals representing 99 species. Next walk northwest past the oryxes and nyalas to Africa, home of the World of Darkness, the Himalayan Highlands, the World of Reptiles, and the Baboon Reserve, which re-creates the Ethiopian highland habitat of the gelada baboon. Walk west past the ostriches and storks to the newest exhibit, the Congo Gorilla Forest, a 6.5-acre indoor/outdoor African rain forest that's home to lowland gorillas, mandrills, African rock pythons, okapis, red river hogs, and colobus monkeys. It's a must-see.

KID-FRIENDLY EATS Snack stands are located throughout the park, selling drinks, ice cream, and every other zoo snack imaginable. For more substantial fare, eat at the **cafeteria, Asia Plaza, Zoo Terrace, African Market** (overlooking the Baboon Reserve), or the **Flamingo Pub.** Tables are available near the cafeteria and Zoo Terrace for those who pack a picnic.

KEEP IN MIND Summer sees the biggest crowds, and many exhibits—the Children's Zoo, Bengali Express, Skyfari, camel rides, and Zoo Shuttle—are open only in warmer months. Not surprisingly, all those human animals, like the animals they've come to see, don't always enjoy the heat. In hot (or cold) weather, visit the indoor, temperature-controlled exhibits. Feeding times make animals active during the day. Sea lions eat at 10:30 and 3, penguins at 3:30. Or come in fall. Strollers are a must, and rentals—including those for adults—are available.

BROOKLYN ACADEMY OF MUSIC

The Brooklyn Academy of Music (BAM), one of America's oldest performing arts centers, presents a full schedule of traditional and contemporary performing arts in the fields of dance, music, theater, musical theater, and opera. The Department of Education and Humanities offers exceptional performances for schoolchildren through the Generation BAM and kaBam series.

The BAMfamily series presents weekend performances for parents and children to enjoy in beautiful theaters, all at affordable prices. This great introduction to dance, music, and theater appeals to tots and teens alike. Performances are chosen to meet several criteria, including cultural diversity, multidisciplinary appeal, exposure to theatrical innovation, and the extent to which the performance is likely to introduce a young audience to art forms they may not have had the opportunity to experience before.

HEY, KIDS! It's time to brush up on your foreign languages. Part of the fun of the BAMkids Film Festival is watching movies from other lands. A recent festival schedule listed live-action and animated films from France, Mozambique, Brazil, Ethiopia, Mexico, Germany, Sweden, Northern Ireland, and Norway. But don't worry if you can't speak the language. Many foreign films have English subtitles, and for most of these films at the festival, the subtitles are read out loud by actors.

 30 Lafayette Ave., Brooklyn

 Concerts $10

718/636–4100, 718/623–2770
film festival

Year-round; call for schedule

5 and up, film festival 4–13

The Brooklyn Academy of Music also presents an annual BAMkids Film Festival, in the main building's BAM Rose Cinemas. Offerings range from animated shorts of four to seven minutes to feature films running 1½ to two hours.

Created in 1908, BAM's main building is the home of three performance spaces: the 2,000-seat Opera House, the 1,000-seat Helen Owen Carey Playhouse, and the multipurpose Lepercq Space, also called "the black box." In October 1987, after extensive renovation, the 900-seat historic Majestic Theater, located two blocks from the main facility at 651 Fulton Street, was opened and is now called the BAM Harvey Theater. But whichever theater you attend, the academy's performances will take your family on artistic journeys of amazing impact. Bam!

TRANSPORTATION To reach BAM by car, take the Manhattan Bridge to Flatbush Avenue. Turn left onto Fulton Street and right onto Ashland Place. BAM parking is one block ahead on the right. (Hint: it's cheaper for subscribers and Friends of BAM.) If you're coming by subway, take the 2, 3, 4, 5, D, or Q line to Atlantic Avenue; the B, N, R, or M line to Pacific Street; or the A or C line to Lafayette Street.

BROOKLYN BOTANIC GARDEN

It's easy to spend a day in this 52-acre blooming paradise with over 12,000 plants outside and under glass. In fact, it's easy to spend several days a year. There's something different to see each season: the Zen-like tranquillity of the Japanese Hill and Pond Garden in fall, the puffy white winter pussy willows and early bulbs bursting with color in the Rock Garden in February, a spring flowering festival of tulips, and sunny summer garden delights.

Among areas specifically for kids is the aptly named, renovated Children's Garden. The oldest of its kind, it's been a prototype for children's gardens around the world. Since 1914, this 1-acre plot has been tended by more than 15,000 young gardeners, who plant, care for, and harvest their own flowers, herbs, and vegetables.

The Discovery Garden is another outdoor adventure for kids, especially preschoolers, but filled with fun for everyone. Your children can look through "bug-eye" lenses or blaze a trail through a bamboo forest, a meadow, maze, grassy areas, and a nature trail.

HEY, KIDS! Check out Amazing Plants!, an exhibit in the Chase Manhattan Discovery Center. In this re-creation of the amazingly diverse borough of Brooklyn, you'll learn how plants survive in the city. The whole exhibit is interactive, and the hands-on activities are really neat. See how seeds travel, how a plant protects itself, and just how tough urban plants can be. The exhibit is for all ages, but you'll find it especially fun if you're between 6 and 12.

 1000 Washington Ave., Brooklyn

718/623–7200, 718/623–7220
Discovery Programs

 $3 adults, 50¢
children 6–16, T free

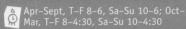 Apr–Sept, T–F 8–6, Sa–Su 10–6; Oct–
Mar, T–F 8–4:30, Sa–Su 10–4:30

All ages

Brightly colored Plant Discovery carts are stocked with games, puzzles, art supplies, and natural objects. (Topics and activities change regularly.) Carts also dispense free Family Fun kits for more exploration at home. Other favorite places in the botanical garden include the Fragrance Garden and the Celebrity Path, whose paving stones are inscribed with the names of famous Brooklynites past and present. How many can you recognize? The Japanese Hill and Pond Garden is home to ducks, turtles, koi, and herons, which can be surveyed from the Viewing Pavilion. The Waiting House, shrines, bridges, and waterfalls complete a miniaturized landscape that appeals to children.

For a more hands-on approach, consider the Discovery Programs: Sunday workshops for 5–12 year-olds (preregistration needed) and 15-minute drop-in workshops on Tuesday for 3–5 year-olds. Topics change monthly, and sessions are held in the Discovery Garden or the Chase Manhattan Discovery Center.

KID-FRIENDLY EATS The garden's **Terrace Cafe** offers lunch on the Spencer Terrace April–October and in the Steinhardt Conservatory November–March. For deli sandwiches and cheesecake, visit **Junior's Restaurant** (386 Flatbush Ave., tel. 718/852–5257), a classic '50s diner. Also *see* the Brooklyn Museum of Art, Prospect Park, and Prospect Park Wildlife Center.

KEEP IN MIND Special family events occur all year long. The fall Chili Pepper Fiesta often includes puppet shows, strolling mariachis, interactive storytelling, paper crafts, and face painting. The Cherry Blossom Festival fairly blooms with activities for children in spring, often including musical performances, martial-arts demonstrations, haiku readings, Japanese storytelling, Japanese printing workshops, doll-making, origami, and calligraphy. In addition, the garden collaborates with the Brooklyn Children's Museum (*see below*) on its horticultural exhibits, including an interactive greenhouse and an exhibit titled Plants and People.

BROOKLYN CHILDREN'S MUSEUM

E nter through a corrugated metal tunnel lit with neon bands, and you immediately know you're on your way to an innovative, educational, fun, and fabulous place for kids. Of course that's not how you would have entered the world's first museum for children when it was founded in 1899. Over the years, this century-old museum has served as a model for other children's museums worldwide, thanks to interactive exhibits, kids' programs, workshops, and performances.

Upon arrival, check the daily information board to see what workshops and programs are planned. Then head to any of the 10 galleries, which incorporate musical traditions, storytelling, science and nature experiments, collections, and computers to create exhibits that tickle the imaginations of young and old.

On any given day, your children may be able to assemble an 8-foot-high elephant skeleton puzzle, play musical instruments from around the world, pet a snake from the live animal

KID-FRIENDLY EATS For plentiful home cooking, try the **New Prospect Cafe** (393 Flatbush Ave., tel. 718/638–2148). The **Lemongrass Grill** (61A 7th Ave., tel. 718/399–7100) is a link in a reasonably priced Thai food chain. Also *see* the Brooklyn Museum of Art.

KEEP IN MIND Look for Early Learners Performances, special music and dance programs held the first weekend of every month for children 5 and younger. Science, creative play, and art workshops for early learners take place the third weekend of each month. Workshops are held Saturday and Sunday 10–11:30 and cost $5 per session. Free Friday Family Fun offers dance and theater performances every Friday evening during the summer.

145 Brooklyn Ave., Brooklyn

718/735-4400

Suggested donation $3

2 and up

collection, or experiment with plants in the greenhouse. Highlights of the museum's 27,000-object permanent collection range from masks, sculpture, instruments, and adornments from African, Central American, Asian, and Oceanic cultures to such natural history specimens as dinosaur footprints, mammoth teeth, an elephant skeleton, and a whale rib. A famous collection of dolls runs the gamut from folk dolls to a 36-piece set of Queen Elizabeth II coronation dolls designed by Madame Alexander.

Your kids can take an imaginary "walk" in over 400 shoes, featured in the exhibition Global Shoes, and can experience and explore various cultures through dance, work, and play. Visit the popular music studio, and be sure to try the "walk-on piano." Even adults can't resist. The new Learning Early Gallery is dedicated to early learning for toddlers, and three theaters include an outdoor rooftop amphitheater where performances from around the world are regularly featured. You might have noticed a strong global emphasis here; along with focusing on a wealth of cultures, this place offers a world of fun.

HEY, KIDS! You'll feel right at home in Together in the City, an exhibit focusing on urban life and discovering cultural traditions. Within the larger exhibit is Celebration Station, where you can build a clubhouse, decorate a parade float, or take a virtual subway ride to Yankee Stadium or New Year's in Chinatown. It's all part of exploring the ways in which people of all backgrounds play, work, and celebrate together in New York City.

BROOKLYN MUSEUM OF ART

It's the second-largest museum in New York State, established in 1823, and considered one of the premier art institutions in the world. Is it in Manhattan? No, it was born and bred—and still lives—in Brooklyn! It's the Beaux Arts–style Brooklyn Museum of Art. Over 1.5 million objects range from the art of ancient Egypt to contemporary painting and sculpture, and the museum's collections of Asian, American, Egyptian, Native American, and African art are recognized as some of the best in the world.

There are all kinds of ways to enjoy the museum with children. If you're bound for the African Galleries, pick up a "Family Guide" at the information desk to help explain what you'll see. Arty Facts is a weekend program for young children and their adult friends that manages to fit a gallery exploration, a family activity, and an art activity into 1½ hours. Other weekend family programs, which are free, include storytelling by guests from around the world; special dance, opera, and other music performances; and meet-the-author or -illustrator seminars. During the school year, weeklong programs are conducted for grade schoolers.

HEY, KIDS! At the Learning Center, explore the Brooklyn Expedition (www.brooklynexpedition.org), a nifty Web site developed by this museum, the Brooklyn Children's Museum, and the Brooklyn Public Library. Containing pictures and articles about objects, exhibits, and collections plus interactive activities, it helps you uncover the three institutions' resources. Once you're back at home or school—or if you can only make a virtual museum visit—you can access the site for help on projects or just for fun. Your museum experience need never end.

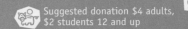

The Gallery/Studio Program offers students the opportunity to study the museum's diverse collections as well as work in the studio on their own art. Courses in drawing, painting, sculpture, abstract art, printmaking, collage, and mixed media are offered in 10-week sessions.

At the Learning Center, located in the first-floor Education Gallery, you and your children can browse in the museum's children's books and CD-ROMS. Outdoors, your kids may be interested by the Frieda Schiff Warburg Memorial Sculpture Garden, which consists of architectural fragments of demolished and famous New York buildings, including the old Penn Station. As your children will discover, there's a lot more to do here than simply wander around looking at paintings, though they'll probably find that pretty special, too.

KID-FRIENDLY EATS The **Museum Café** is open almost as long as the museum, or try the **Second Street Cafe** (see the Prospect Park Wildlife Center). For a snack and a warm drink, try **Ozzie's Coffee & Tea** (57 7th Ave., tel. 718/ 398–6695). Your kids will find this converted drugstore with apothecary cases an interesting spot for juice or tea.

KEEP IN MIND The museum is near the Brooklyn Botanic Garden (see above), the main branch of the Brooklyn Public Library, and Prospect Park and its wildlife center (see below). Although you could easily spend a day at the museum, it's probably better, especially with young children, to keep your first visit short. Spend half a day here, wander to 7th Avenue for lunch at one of the restaurants and cafés, and visit another nearby destination in the afternoon. It'll break up the day and leave your children with a good memory of the museum.

CARNEGIE HALL

How do you get to Carnegie Hall? Practice... Practice... or just attend one of the family concerts held throughout the year on Saturday afternoons on this world-famous stage. The family concert series, begun in 1995, introduces children to classical, jazz, and folk music at affordable, family-friendly prices. Pre-concert activities on the main stage and in other smaller Carnegie Hall spaces include storytelling, hands-on musical experiences, and instrument demonstrations. Concert-goers also receive a special "KidsBill" program specially designed for youngsters, with activities and information about each family concert.

Another wonderful concert program called Carnegie*KIDS* is designed to introduce music to preschool children. It's available to nursery schools, day care centers, kindergarten classes, Headstart programs, and small groups by advance reservation. These concerts are not held in the main hall, however, but rather in the Kaplan space on the fifth floor.

HEY, KIDS!
If you're a movie buff, you may remember that *Home Alone 2* takes place in New York City and that the lady who feeds the pigeons lives in the attic of—you guessed it— Carnegie Hall! Of course, there's no truth to the rumor that she still lives here. That's only in the movies.

KEEP IN MIND Can't get to Carnegie Hall? Let Carnegie Hall come to you! Since 1976, the Neighborhood Concert Series has hosted concerts in public libraries, community and senior centers, and shelters in all five New York City boroughs. These free, one-hour concerts are part of an outreach program jointly sponsored by the city's Department of Cultural Affairs. A variety of artists and ensembles performing repertoires from classical and jazz to folk and pop make up each Neighborhood Concert season. Seating is on a first-come, first-served basis.

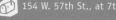

 154 W. 57th St., at 7th Ave.

 Family concerts under $7;
CarnegieKIDS $3; tour $6 adults, $5
students, $3 children 11 and under

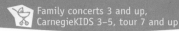 Tour M–T and Th–F 11:30, 2, and 3,
performances permitting

212/247–7800

Family concerts 3 and up,
CarnegieKIDS 3–5, tour 7 and up

To make a concert experience special for children, it might help to discuss any famous musicians that you or other family members saw perform here. Headliners have been playing Carnegie Hall since 1891, when its opening concert series included none other than Tchaikovsky conducting his own works. Since then, the hall has attracted the world's finest orchestras and solo and group performers, from Arturo Toscanini and Leonard Bernstein to Duke Ellington, Ella Fitzgerald, Judy Garland, Frank Sinatra, Bob Dylan, and the Beatles, who played one of their first U.S. concerts here.

One-hour guided tours of the hall are also available. And if your kids want to get a close-up look at Benny Goodman's clarinet or catch a glimpse of Arturo Toscanini's baton, visit the Rose Museum Thursday through Tuesday or during concert intermissions. East of the main auditorium, this small museum displays an interesting array of mementos from Carnegie Hall's rich history.

KID-FRIENDLY EATS After a concert, whistle a happy tune over to **Serendipity 3** (22 E. 60th St., tel. 212/838–3531). Popular kid fare includes foot-long hot dogs, burgers, and fries, or just come for the famous and fabulous desserts: Serendipity's sumptuous sundaes and fantastic frozen hot chocolate. You can order a mile-high sandwich or classic cheesecake at the famous **Carnegie Deli** (854 7th Ave., tel. 212/757–2245).

CASTLE CLINTON NATIONAL MONUMENT

Like any good castle, Castle Clinton has a long and varied history. It was built shortly before the beginning of the War of 1812 to defend New York City from sea assault, but no attack ever came. Today you can admire the beautiful views of the Statue of Liberty and Ellis Island along with the park landscape all around, while your children can enjoy looking for gun turrets and scanning the stone walls, imagining themselves soldiers defending a city.

Originally named the South-west Battery, this circular redbrick fortress served as U.S. Army headquarters during the War of 1812. It had a timber causeway with a drawbridge connecting the fort to Manhattan and was equipped with 28 guns and a magazine inside the rounded ends of the rear wall. National Park Service rangers dressed in period costume are available to answer questions, and a room features dioramas and exhibits that tell of this setting's many lives.

It's hard to imagine a more varied history. In 1824 the site was turned into an elegant entertainment and concert facility known as Castle Garden, where the "Swedish Nightingale,"

HEY, KIDS! How did the location and design of Castle Clinton help guard the coast of our young country? Notice that Castle Williams, on Governor's Island, is opposite Castle Clinton. Why were these two forts built so near each other? And why do you think Castle Clinton is designed in the shape of a capital D, a circle flattened on the land side? If enemy ships were moving up the East River, how could Castle Clinton help stop this attack?

Jenny Lind, sang in 1850. From 1855 to 1890, it served as a receiving station for more than 8 million immigrants and from 1896 to 1941 housed the New York Aquarium. Today it functions as a restored fort, museum, and ticket office for ferries to the Statue of Liberty and Ellis Island.

Look for the bronze statue titled *The Immigrants,* depicting a Jewish man bent in prayer with his family, along with a priest, a freed African-American slave, a worker, and a child. Paying homage to the immigrants who passed through here, it's at the beginning of a wide expanse that leads to the Netherlands Memorial Flagpole, which commemorates a different era of the site's history—the Dutch purchase of the land for Fort Amsterdam from Native Americans. Inscriptions of this historic event are sculpted into the pedestal in English and Dutch. In all, over 300 years of history can be discovered here in Battery Park.

KID-FRIENDLY EATS Check out the kid-friendly eateries suggested in listings for Fraunces Tavern Museum, New York Unearthed, the South Street Seaport Museum, and the Statue of Liberty.

KEEP IN MIND Castle Clinton is only one of six historic National Park Service units in New York City. The others include Federal Hall National Memorial and the Theodore Roosevelt Birthplace (*see below*), St. Paul's National Historic Site, General Grant National Memorial, and the Hamilton Grange National Memorial. In addition to its other functions, Castle Clinton is a visitor center for the city's national parks.

CENTRAL PARK

Central Park is to New York as the sun is to the solar system. This green oasis of over 840 acres is a magnet for families, joggers, bikers, strollers (on foot and wheels), skaters, sunbathers, and people-watchers. Where else in the city can you go horseback riding, boating, ice-skating, roller skating, folk dancing, fishing, and bird-watching; visit the zoo; and attend a play, puppet show, concert, and ball game—though probably not in one day? Weekends are busy here (but crowds make it safe), and free entertainment is everywhere you look.

A good starting point is the Dairy (64th St., mid-park, tel. 212/794-6564), whose exhibits and interactive videos provide an introduction. Grab a map and calendar of events. Looking for playgrounds? Head to 67th Street and 5th Avenue for the tree house playground. Others are located on the east side at 71st, 77th, 85th, and 95th streets and on the west side at 68th, 85th, 93rd, and 96th streets.

HEY, KIDS!
Though the park isn't even 150 years old, you can find attractions spanning several millennia. On the old side, Cleopatra's Needle, a hieroglyphic-covered obelisk east of the Great Lawn near the Metropolitan Museum of Art, dates to 1600 BC. In 1881 Egypt gave it to New York City.

KEEP IN MIND It's not just couples who like horse-drawn carriage rides. Kids love them, too. You'll see the carriages assembled on Central Park South (59th Street between 5th Avenue and Central Park West). Each is decorated distinctively, and the drivers, too, are a colorful group. Some even sport top hats. Day and evening rides are available for about $35 for 20 minutes. As long as you're home by midnight, the carriage won't turn into a pumpkin and your little Cinderella will stay queen of the ball!

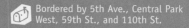 Bordered by 5th Ave., Central Park West, 59th St., and 110th St.

 Free; some attractions charge

 Daily sunrise–sunset

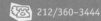 212/360-3444

All ages

On park land: Take a ride on the 1903 Friedsam Memorial Carousel (Center Dr. and 65th St., tel. 212/879–0244), the second-oldest on the East Coast. Belvedere Castle (79th St. Transverse, tel. 212/772–0210), home of a weather station and the Henry Luce Nature Observatory, houses nature exhibits, children's workshops, and educational programs. Marionette performances are held at the nearby Swedish Cottage (79th St. Transverse, tel. 212/988–9093), an 1876 schoolhouse.

On or near park waters: Snap a photo at Conservatory Water (between 5th Ave. and East Dr.), where children pose by literary statues. Summer storytelling hours take place Saturday at 11, while model boats race Saturday at 10 spring–fall. At the Charles A. Dana Discovery Center (5th Ave. and 110th St.), you can borrow free poles and bait and head to Harlem Meer (5th Ave. and 110th St., tel. 212/860–1370) for catch-and-release fishing. To skate on frozen water, try the Wollman Memorial Rink (6th Ave. at 59th St., tel. 212/396–1010), mid-October–March (in-line skating April–September). Tired yet?

KID-FRIENDLY EATS Try the **Loeb Boathouse Cafe** (*see* the Central Park Wildlife Center), a seasonal open-air restaurant on the water, or a nearby cafeteria serving breakfast and lunch. For a splurge, visit famous **Tavern on the Green** (Central Park West at 67th St., tel. 212/873–3200). Twinkling lights, glitzy glass, and mirrors captivate young audiences. Pre-theater specials are reasonable, but reservations are a must.

CENTRAL PARK WILDLIFE CENTER

56

By 1864, captive animals could be found in Central Park. (Of course wild animals were here earlier, as they are today—with varying numbers of feet.) In 1934, this Animal Menagerie was remodeled, becoming the first Central Park Zoo. It was renovated again in 1980, this time by the Wildlife Conservation Society, an international conservation organization, which now operates it as the Central Park Wildlife Center—at least that's its official name. Approximately 450 animals represent over 100 species in the 5½-acre zoo, a perfect destination for little ones. It's walkable and stroller-friendly, and even the youngest tot can see the animals from low-lying or low-sitting carriages. Three climatic regions—the Tropic Zone, Temperate Territory, and Polar Circle—form the focal points.

The Tropic Zone is a veritable jungle, filled with the sounds and swirling mist of a roaring waterfall and the calls of tropical birds. Older children like the piranha aquarium and the ant nest, containing over 100,000 leaf-cutter ants. A way-cool sight in the Temperate Territory is an island of Japanese snow monkeys in a lake with black-neck swans.

HEY, KIDS! Did you know the sea lion pool holds 100,000 gallons of water? (Sea lions need a lot of space to swim around in, so, no, it wouldn't be a good idea to keep one in your bathtub.) Check out the glass panels for below-the-water views of their swimming antics, and try to get here at 11:30, 2, or 4. That's when they're fed. It's too much fun to miss.

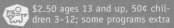
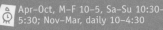

Speaking of cool, the Polar Circle contains some exhibits refrigerated to 34°. Look for arctic foxes as well as the ever-popular penguins, puffins, and polar bears, whose natural habitats feature 10 viewing areas with above- and below-water views.

In the Tisch Children's Zoo, children can explore touch boxes, hear through huge rabbit ears, examine giant turtle shells and eggs, observe waterfowl from behind a child-size duck blind, and pet and feed many animals. Small animal sculptures moo, baa, or grunt when touched by little hands.

Costumed animal characters mingle with visitors, answering (and posing) questions. The Acorn Theater presents shows using puppets, costumed characters, music, and song to teach basic animal facts. Where else could you hear the "Metamorphosis Boogie" or participate in a Wildlife Workout? Something tells me it's all happening at the, er, wildlife center.

KID-FRIENDLY EATS Kids go wild for snacks at the zoo's indoor-outdoor **Cafe.** Central Park also has food stands near many entrances. You may recognize the pricey **Loeb Boathouse Cafe** (East Park Dr. and E. 72nd St., tel. 212/517–2233) from such movies as *Three Men and a Little Lady* and *Postcards from the Edge;* open March–September.

KEEP IN MIND Special community events like National Pig Day, Creature Courtship Day, and Chill Out with the Polar Bears and Penguins are scheduled throughout the year, free with general admission. An interactive preschool series for children 3–5 with an adult is offered for a fee in various sessions throughout the year. Children's and family programs (some with charges) for youngsters 6 and up have included such favorites as Breakfast with the Birds, Snooze at the Zoo, Rainforest Retreat, and Spooky Species.

CHELSEA PIERS

It has been called Manhattan's ultimate playground with spectacular views. Chelsea Piers opened in 1995 as a riverside recreation resort featuring bowling, basketball, soccer, in-line skating, swimming, sailing, kayaking, and rock climbing. As incongruous as it sounds, your family can ice-skate in summer and play golf all winter, all on piers jutting into the Hudson River. The piers date back to 1910, part of a grand row of nine piers that were a popular port of call for many grand transatlantic ocean liners. In 1994 the Chelsea Piers were restored and revitalized, and construction of the state-of-the-art complex began.

The first thing to do, of course, is to pick an activity. The Field House (between Piers 61 and 62, tel. 212/336–6500) is an 80,000-square-foot facility for gymnastics, team sports, basketball, soccer, and lacrosse. It contains four batting cages, dance studios, a martial arts mezzanine, and a climbing wall designed for children, teens, and adult beginners. There are open gym and open toddler gym sessions as well as open climbing. Sky Rink (Pier 61, tel. 212/336–6100) is open 24/seven, just in case you feel the need to ice-skate at 3 AM.

HEY, KIDS!
Check out one of the best vert ramps and street courses in the country at the Skate Park at the Roller Rinks. Here you can safely "launch and grind!" You can also choose from two regulation-size outdoor rinks or a skate school offering in-line instruction, if roller-skating is your thing.

KEEP IN MIND At the 1¼-mile Waterside Promenade you can stroll, grab a bench, picnic at tables, or just relax and enjoy the spectacular Hudson River views. Free summer concerts and community events take place at the tip of Pier 62 at Pier Park. But if you decide to take a walk while your kids pursue other activities (younger children, of course, should be kept with you), plan to meet up later at a specific time at an agreed-upon, no-fail place. As this recreational mecca is a vast space, without a plan, you could be pacing the piers for hours.

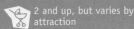
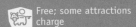
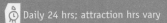
AMF Chelsea Piers Bowl (between Piers 59 and 60, tel. 212/835–BOWL) is a 40-lane, state-of-the-art facility equipped with automatic scoring, bumper bowling for kids, and Xtreme Bowling, an evening bowling experience with black lights, Day-Glo pins, music, and fog machines. A Golf Center (Pier 59, tel. 212/336–6400) houses 52 heated and weather-protected hitting stalls on four levels with a computerized automatic ball tee-up system. You and your children can practice year-round or take lessons or classes from pros.

Like the city it's in, Chelsea Piers has something for everyone—adults, kids, New Yorkers, and visitors. And if you lack the equipment, you can rent or buy everything you need here for an extraordinary visit to this 30-acre sports village.

KID-FRIENDLY EATS Three restaurants offer on-site dining. **Rita's Burgers** (Sunset Strip at Pier 60, tel. 212/336–6299), a blend of city chic and country comfort, serves beef, turkey, tuna, and veggie burgers. For seafood and river views, try the **Crab House** (Pier 61, tel. 212/835–CRAB), whose Captain Kidd's menu is just for kids. **Chelsea Brewing Company** (Pier 59, tel. 212/336–6440), overlooking the marina, features casual riverside pub fare indoors or out. Or just picnic along the promenade.

CHILDREN'S MUSEUM OF THE ARTS

It's hard to know where to begin when entering this small SoHo museum, but somehow children manage. They set their own pace, find a space that interests them, and move on, often returning to their favorite workshop or exhibit. The focus here is hands-on art, based on the theory that children learn best by doing. And they do . . . and do. In 5,000 square feet of kid-comfortable space, they touch, create, and explore.

Your children can draw on a computerized sketch pad and then see their work on a TV monitor, developing computer skills, artistic sensibilities, and hand-eye coordination without even realizing it. Magnetic Masterpieces turns famous paintings into puzzles. Here you and your kids can piece together large-format reproduction art puzzles; background information about the artists and time period gives you something to talk about as you work.

For the older half of the kids who come here, the Artist's Studio features daily art projects involving problem solving and exploration with a variety of art materials. It's not unusual

KID-FRIENDLY EATS
In the mood for waffles any time of day? Visit the **Cupping Room Cafe** (359 W. Broadway, tel. 212/925–2898). Weekend brunch is also a treat. For a hip, moderately priced artist hangout, try **Jerry's** (101 Prince St., tel. 212/966–9464).

HEY, KIDS!
Need to shake the sillies out? Jump into the Ball Pond, a carpeted area filled with large, brightly colored physioballs. The theory behind it is that the kinesthetic experience fosters motor-skill play, but you'll probably just think that it's a great place to get started in the museum. Thanks to the creative use of color, light, and texture, the surrounding area gives the illusion of being underwater. So dive right in!

182 Lafayette St.

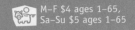 M–F $4 ages 1–65,
Sa–Su $5 ages 1–65

212/274–0986

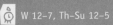 W 12–7, Th–Su 12–5

 1–10, Artist's Studio 6 and over,
Creative Play Area 4 and under

to find artists from the community working side-by-side with the next artistic generation here. Meanwhile, the younger half can enjoy the Creative Play Area, which includes an Art Station, where the art projects are designed for sensory stimulation. The area's Colorform Wall is a glass window where children manipulate a variety of shapes, and its Art House is a small two-story space with slide shows and costumes for pretend play.

Ongoing workshops in music, dance, theater, puppetry, and visual arts foster skill mastery, open-ended exploration, and creativity, thus instilling confidence in children. Paintings, sculptures, and drawings from museum visitors, adult artists, and children from around the world are displayed in workshop areas throughout the museum. Along with the permanent collection, a number of special exhibitions and temporary displays are also hung throughout the year. Big things are created in a small space by little people with huge imaginations.

KEEP IN MIND The Children's Museum of the Arts conducts programs at the museum especially geared to special-needs children, their families, and schools. In addition, a School and Community Outreach Program serves over 10,000 children and their families at schools, settlement houses, and special needs facilities.

CHILDREN'S MUSEUM OF
MANHATTAN

Where do burps come from? How do you stop bleeding? Where does dead skin go? For the answers and for an unforgettable journey through the human body, visit the interactive Body Odyssey exhibit. Here you can visit a blood tunnel, where you and your children can experience the sensation of flowing through large fabricated blood vessels bathed in light. You can climb onto a giant tongue and work your way through the digestive system, shooting stomach acid and helping food churn through the intestines. Or watch as your children fight body invaders and command immune protectors in educational computer games. Geared toward youngsters 5 and up and their parents, this health and wellness exhibit is a highlight of this museum that stimulates the imagination, invites exploration, and encourages creativity and learning in fabulously fun and challenging ways.

If you're here with a younger child, try WordPlay, an exhibit for children under 4. Developed in response to research on stimulation in children's early years, it focuses on language development and literacy and comprises seven engaging environments designed to build cognitive, social,

HEY, KIDS! If you're 6 or older, visit the Time Warner Media Center, the only production studio of its kind in the city. Here you can be part of CD-ROM-TV, working either on camera or behind the scenes. Techies can operate cameras, edit videos, or experiment with state-of-the-art equipment even grown-ups usually can't touch. If you'd rather be "on the air," you can read the news, do the weather with meteorologists' maps and equipment, or take part in the museum's news magazine.

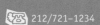 Tisch Building, 212 W. 83rd St.

212/721–1234

 $5 ages 1 and up

 W–Su 10–5

1–10

and physical skills. Baby Babble is a multisensory area for the very youngest visitors. Explorers' Park features a twisting textured path for crawlers and toddlers. Apartment ABC is a child-size apartment mixing fantasy and reality, and Chatterbug Tree allows climbers to become a bird or squirrel. At the Post Office Pick-up, little ones sort letters and words and take a ride on the mail truck. Readers' Pond is the site for storytelling and book-based programs, and the Resource Nook provides parents and caregivers with the latest research on early childhood education and development.

Elsewhere, ongoing art classes meet in the Russell Berrie Art Studio. The Book of the Week Program takes place in the Helena Rubinstein Literacy Center. Children 18 months to 4 years can climb, slide, paint, and sing in the intimate Early Childhood Center and Creative Corner. There's always something cooking, figuratively—sometimes even literally—at CMOM. See, Mom! It's worth missing a nap!

KID-FRIENDLY EATS Try the kid-size portions or the family-style meat loaf served whole at **Main Street** (446 Columbus Ave., tel. 212/873–5025). For chili, burgers, and gooey desserts, sample the food at **Firehouse** (522 Columbus Ave., tel. 212/595–3139).

KEEP IN MIND The museum is undergoing a major expansion, but that hasn't curtailed the nonstop fun and festivities that happen daily here. Sing-alongs, Step into Story Adventures, memory books to make and take, TV production workshops, and Word Wizard performances are just a few of the programs that could be in store for you. Call ahead to hear what's scheduled for the day you visit, or check the posted schedule of events as soon as you arrive. Then head first to the areas that pique your child's interest the most.

CLAY PIT PONDS STATE PARK PRESERVE

ew York City's only state park preserve, these 260 natural acres near Staten Island's southwest shore were once the site of a clay-mining operation (hence the name). But to really tell its history, you have to go back to the Cretaceous period, nearly 70 million years ago, when sands and clays were deposited here. More recent glacial deposits, 12,000 years ago, add to the area's geological significance. Evidence of Leni Lenape Indians, European settlers, and the Free Blacks of Sandy Ground, who arrived from Maryland in the early 1800s, adds a cultural thread to the land's rich tapestry. But though the visitor center does have historical photos and a few artifacts, the main draw here is nature.

Established in 1977, the preserve harbors such diverse habitats as fields, sandy barrens, spring-fed streams, bogs and other freshwater wetlands, and woodlands, creating an oasis amid an urban area and enabling city dwellers to commune with nature. Each season paints a different natural backdrop. Throughout the year, wildflowers or their dried silhouettes can be seen along the trails. White wild carrot flowers and Queen Anne's lace frame summer fields, folding

HEY, KIDS! Get a trail guide and look at its illustrations so you can identify the plants and animals you see on the preserve. Can you find a screech owl, box turtle, fence lizard, raccoon, or black-capped chickadee? In addition to helping put names to flora and fauna, the trail guide will alert you to landscape changes. Also look for structures, like steps or bridges, and trail markers, and remember not to disturb, destroy, or collect anything along your journey.

up in winter to resemble tiny birds' nests. The wildflower garden behind headquarters is particularly colorful in spring, though some flowers blossom in late summer. Ask for a key to identify the garden's contents.

For a more "cultivated" experience, head to the organic vegetable garden, chicken coop, berry patch, weather station, or beehives. Hiking and horseback riding are permitted on designated trails. Take the Abraham's Pond Trail (blue markers) to the Ellis Swamp Trail (yellow markers) for a 1-mile walk, or stay on the Abraham's Pond Trail the entire way, a ½-mile jaunt.

Free educational programming goes beyond guided and self-guided nature walks to cover pond ecology, bird-watching, tree and wildflower identification, organic gardening, and beekeeping. Evening campfires and special children's programs round out the experience for the whole family.

KID-FRIENDLY EATS There are picnic tables behind preserve headquarters. German fare is on tap at **Killmeyer's** (4254 Arthur Kill Rd., tel. 718/984–1202). The fixed-price lunch is a bargain, and evenings often bring an oompah band. The 1716 **Old Bermuda Inn** (2512 Arthur Kill Rd., tel. 718/948–7600) costs more for lunch and dinner, but the weekend brunch is a good value.

KEEP IN MIND Trails are for feet or hooves only. Neither tires (bicycles) nor paws (dogs and other pets) are permitted. Keep an eye out for nonpoisonous snakes. Your children may be startled by the garter, black racer, and water snakes that live here, but you can assure them that they pose no threat to us—only to the insect and rodent populations they keep in check.

COLDEN CENTER FOR THE
PERFORMING ARTS

Since 1961, the Colden Center for the Performing Arts at Queens College has been presenting world-class performing artists in the fields of music, dance, theater, jazz, popular entertainment, children's and family programming, and arts education. Performances can be seen at the 475-seat Irving and Susan Wallack Goldstein Theatre; the Samuel J. and Ethel LeFrak Concert Hall, a 489-seat state-of-the-art recital hall with recording studio; or the Colden Auditorium, which seats 2,143 and boasts excellent acoustics and sight lines.

KidsClassics concerts are just what they sound like: a series of classical music concerts that involve children as active listeners. An eclectic musical menu augmented by audience participation captivates both young and old. Before the concerts, families can create their own musical instruments and add their artwork to the portable gallery.

Family Theatre performances might include such universal favorites as the *Nutcracker* ballet, American Family Theatre's *Alice in Wonderland,* or a special musical afternoon with

KID-FRIENDLY EATS For excellent, cheap noodle soup, try the Vietnamese restaurant **Pho Bang** (41-07 Kissena Blvd., tel. 718/939–5520). For cheap, fast, and hearty authentic Cantonese dishes, dine at the **Sweet-n-Tart Cafe** (136-11 38th Ave., tel. 718/661–3380).

KEEP IN MIND Call the Queens College Arts Hotline (tel. 718/997–ARTS) to see what else is happening on campus. The Godwin–Ternbach Museum's collection comprises over 2,500 artworks, and four major exhibitions are mounted annually. The Queens College Art Center's Benjamin S. Rosenthal Library exhibits modern and contemporary art. The Louis Armstrong Archives contain the great jazz pioneer's recordings, instruments, manuscripts, memorabilia, photographs, and scrapbooks. The college is also working to convert his home into a museum and educational center.

musician and storyteller Tom Chapin. Many events are ideal for all ages; others have age recommendations.

The DanceClassics series introduces young audiences to the world of dance. A beautifully illustrated "Dance Classics Handbook," chock-full of dance concepts, trivia, history, activities, and suggested books for children, is given to young audience members before each performance. A lively question-and-answer session takes place after each performance.

Besides the exceptional programming just for kids, selected all-age special events and individual performances in the fields of dance, music, and theater may also be of interest to your children. Past shows have included comedian Gallagher, 100 Years of Broadway, Dance Theatre of Harlem, Ballet Hispanico of New York, and Pops is Tops, an annual jazz concert series for children. Budding instrumentalists may also be interested in the classical concert series.

HEY, KIDS! The KidsClassics "Classic Talk Program Guide" has really cool activities, puzzles, science experiments, and a musical "road map" to help you get the most out of these classical concerts. Rude Randy and Polite Perry teach concert etiquette. Rap to the beat while you learn about percussion instruments and rhythm, and meet the musical members of the chamber orchestra—the instruments, that is. Try not to peek at the puzzle solutions and activity answers in the back of the book.

CONEY ISLAND

Developed as a seaside resort in the early 19th century, Coney Island became famous as a growing amusement center in the 1880s. By the 1950s, it had begun to decline as an amusement and resort destination but steadily grew as a residential area. Today summer crowds still flock to the boardwalk, the 3-mile beach, a huge amusement park (Astroland), and a seaside aquarium (*see* the New York Aquarium). Fishing on the pier, go-carts, a batting cage, and a sports center offering ice-skating and indoor sports round out the recreational opportunities. On warm and sunny days, you'll find a lively mix here, with summer weekends the busiest times. Apartment dwellers come to escape the stifling summer heat; teenagers come for the thrill rides, and families flock to Coney Island with kids in tow to rekindle a memory and to create new ones for the next generation.

Its glory days may be gone, but Astroland Amusement Park is still a family favorite. The wooden Cyclone roller coaster remains as popular today as it was when it first ran in 1927. A water flume and 14 kiddie rides are also on the amusement menu here. At Deno's Wonder Wheel

HEY, KIDS! Consider this. The Wonder Wheel was built in 1920 (before your grandparents were born?) with Bethlehem steel forged on-site. Standing 150 feet tall (half a football field), it has 16 swinging passenger cars and eight stationary cars and was declared a New York City landmark in 1989. The only time it stopped running was on July 13, 1977, during the infamous New York City blackout. To get the riders down to safety, the owners hand-cranked the huge wheel. Ready to ride?

 Southern tip of Brooklyn; Astroland, W. 8th St. and Surf Ave.; Deno's, W. 12th St.; sideshows, W. 12th St. and Surf Ave.

 Attractions' hrs vary by season

718/855–7882 Brooklyn Tourism Council

Free; Astroland and Deno's $2–$4 per ride; sideshows $3; museum 99¢

 1 and up

Amusement Park, 25 rides, two arcades, and an old-fashioned sweet shop are the main attractions.

Lively traditional circus sideshows, complete with a fire-eater, sword swallower, snake charmer, and contortionist, are featured at Sideshows by the Seashore. Upstairs from the sideshows, you'll find the Coney Island Museum, which contains exhibits spotlighting historic Coney Island and related memorabilia. An extensive array of tourist information and literature is also available here.

Despite all its changes, Coney Island is still probably the closest you'll get to an old-fashioned seaside resort in New York.

KID-FRIENDLY EATS On the boardwalk, you can grab a slice of pizza, an Italian ice, a large pretzel, fried clams, or, better yet, a frank. After all, this is where Nathan's Famous made Coney Island hot dog history. If you're interested in restaurants, *see* those suggested in the New York Aquarium. The aquarium is also on the Coney Island boardwalk.

KEEP IN MIND There are many individual (and sometimes question-able) ride operators up and down the boardwalk outside of Astroland and Deno's. It's advisable to stay in the two-block area between these two amusement parks, using the Nathan's Famous restaurant at Stillwell Avenue as your western marker and the New York Aquarium as your eastern landmark. This area is pleasant, safe, and filled with fun for everyone in your Coney Island caravan. To get even more from your day, park at the aquarium, and spend some time there before or after your amusement park adventure or beach blanket bingo.

ELLIS ISLAND

A symbol of America's immigrant experience, Ellis Island welcomed some 12 million people into the United States from 1892 until 1954. Today their descendants make up almost 40% of the U.S. population, as well as many of the visitors here. Should you choose to join those millions and set foot on this landmark, you can discover or rediscover this important part of American history.

The Ellis Island Immigrant Museum was opened in 1990 to tell the remarkable stories of the immigrants who passed through these buildings. In 200,000 square feet, the museum uses restored areas, educational facilities, and exhibits comprising over 2,000 artifacts—personal papers, jewelry, religious articles, and clothing—to tell tales of countless weary travelers. Enter through the first-floor Baggage Room, through piles of "all their worldly possessions," and view the video presentation, which will help you plan your tour of the more than 30 galleries. (Two award-winning films are shown in theaters on the first and second floors, and a state-of-the-art interactive learning center is accessible by reservation only.)

HEY, KIDS!

Most immigrants who arrived at Ellis Island were fleeing such hardships as poverty, religious persecution, and political unrest in their homelands. Do you have any ancestors who passed through the island? Try speaking to them before your visit or, if they've died, to someone who knows their story.

KID-FRIENDLY EATS Pack a picnic lunch to eat at Ellis Island, or after you return, walk over to the brick plaza behind 85 Broad Street for a takeout meal from any of the area's small restaurants. Children can't go wrong at **T.G.I. Friday's** (47 Broadway, tel. 212/483–8322). Kids' meals come with balloons, crayons, stickers, and souvenir cups. Look for other nearby restaurants in Fraunces Tavern Museum, South Street Seaport Museum, and New York Unearthed.

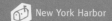 New York Harbor

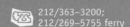 212/363–3200;
212/269–5755 ferry

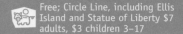 Free; Circle Line, including Ellis
Island and Statue of Liberty $7
adults, $3 children 3–17

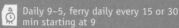 Daily 9–5, ferry daily every 15 or 30
min starting at 9

 8 and up

The next stop, Peopling of America, has 11 graphic displays chronicling four centuries of immigration. View the changing exhibits on the first floor before ascending to the Registry Room of the Great Hall. The hall, where immigrants were questioned and either granted or denied entry, has been restored. The cavernous space with soaring tiled arches seems to echo with the sounds of those hopeful souls.

See the remaining exhibits and facilities on the second and third floors before heading to the unrestored old kitchen and laundry building, which offers a glimpse of what the island's structures looked like before restoration. Lastly, visit the American Immigrant Wall of Honor, where 420,000 immigrant's names are inscribed in steel along an outdoor promenade overlooking the Statue of Liberty and Manhattan skyline. Families can pay to have a name added. Some recognizable names include Miles Standish, Priscilla Alden, and Irving Berlin. It's the largest memorial wall of names in the world, fitting for a nation of immigrants.

TRANSPORTATION The Circle Line ferry sails from Battery Park, South Ferry, at Manhattan's southern tip, and includes a visit to the Statue of Liberty (see below). The trip takes 15 minutes to Liberty Island, 10 minutes from there to Ellis Island, and 10 minutes back to Battery Park. Since reservations aren't accepted, it's good to catch the first boat in the morning to avoid long lines, unavoidable during the busiest times—weekends year-round and every day in summer. Refreshments and souvenirs are sold on board. Once on Ellis Island, you can stay as long as you like—until closing time.

EMPIRE STATE BUILDING

One of the most-recognized and most-photographed buildings in the world, the art deco Empire State Building has towered over the New York skyline since 1931. The 1,454-foot structure with a limestone and granite exterior was built in one year and 45 days for a total of $41 million. (Renovations over the last six years have cost an additional $67 million, well over the original price.) Now a National Historic Landmark, it has been featured in hundreds of films viewed by millions of moviegoers. No wonder that first-time city visitors often make it their first sight-seeing stop! Over 3.5 million people come here each year; the total since 1931 is over 117 million.

After you've purchased tickets on the concourse, one level below ground level, high-speed express elevators whisk you to the 86th-floor observatory in less than a minute. A temperature-controlled, glass-enclosed area offers panoramic views of the city, and you may also take in the sights from a surrounding open-air promenade. Try the on-site high-powered binoculars for a closer view.

HEY, KIDS! The New York Skyride (tel. 888/SKYRIDE), located on the building's second floor, is a big-screen thrill ride that takes you on a one-of-a-kind tour of New York at warp speed. Zoom through F.A.O. Schwarz, crash on Wall Street, and dip into the East River. With the late James Doohan (Scotty from *Star Trek*) as your pilot and comedian Yakov Smirnoff as your copilot—well, you can just imagine. It's the ride of your life, and it runs daily 10–10.

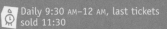

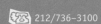 350 5th Ave., at 34th St.

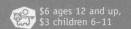 $6 ages 12 and up, $3 children 6–11

 Daily 9:30 AM–12 AM, last tickets sold 11:30

212/736-3100

2 and up

From here, another elevator takes you to even higher heights: the 102nd-floor observation deck. This fully enclosed circular tower offers breathtaking views. Above the observation deck are broadcast and transmission facilities serving 15 FM radio stations and four local TV stations.

On your way out, pause on the 34th Street side of the building to notice the series of eight towering illuminated panels depicting the Seven Wonders of the Ancient World. In 1955 the American Society of Civil Engineers designated the building the Eighth Wonder of the Modern World. Once the tallest building on earth, it's no longer even the tallest building in the city, but that doesn't detract one bit from a trip up this classic early skyscraper.

KID-FRIENDLY EATS On the 86th floor, along with the observatory and a souvenir and gift shop, a snack bar serves light snacks and beverages. The **Metro Grill** (45 W. 35th St., tel. 212/279–3535) is a great place to catch a bite to eat. Also *see* restaurants in Madison Square Garden.

KEEP IN MIND On a clear day you can see forever—well, at least about 80 miles and to five states: New York, New Jersey, Pennsylvania, Connecticut, and Massachusetts. Needless to say, plan to visit on a sunny day. On the other hand, visiting at night has its own allure. Gazing down on the city that never sleeps reveals a sparkling tapestry. The one time you shouldn't come, however, is during inclement weather; save your money and go somewhere else.

F.A.O. SCHWARZ

It's not unusual, especially around the holidays, for lines to stream out the doors and down the sidewalk next to this world-famous and beloved toy store. Walk around the corner past the whimsical window displays and enter on the Madison Avenue side, where lines are often shorter. Find the large mechanical clock tinkling the tune "Welcome to Our World of Toys," and prepare to embark on a fantasy journey into toyland. Two glorious floors of everything from stuffed animals to action figures, games to dolls await the young and the young at heart.

The first-floor stuffed animal collection is one of the most extensive anywhere, with many in the menagerie twice as big as your young shopper. Toys are clustered throughout the store in small boutiques. Visit the Barbie Boutique for anything and everything under the sun for your little one's collection.

Lego-lovers sit for hours at the Lego table, constructing the most intricate buildings and feats of engineering. Your kids will probably climb in the cozy kid automobile on the

KID-FRIENDLY EATS

For scrumptious desserts, salad bar, sandwiches, and antipasto, eat at **Mangia** (50 W. 57th St., tel. 212/582–5882). For a frightfully fun meal, eat at **Jekyll & Hyde** (1409 6th Ave., tel. 212/541–9505), where special effects are more special than the cuisine.

KEEP IN MIND

Compare prices beforehand, so you know by exactly how much you're overpaying. There are no great bargains to be had here price-wise, but you can't beat the selection. Search out the hottest toys on the store's Web site (www.faoschwarz.com), and discuss spending limits ahead of time. With an older child, you might even use a store visit as a lesson in basic economics. Compare prices together, and decide how best to be savvy shoppers. But since most youngsters are acquisitive as well as inquisitive, it's realistic to expect that you'll leave the store with a toy (or two) in tow.

 767 5th Ave., at 58th St.

 M–Sa 10–6, Su 11–6

 212/644–9400

 Free (theoretically)

1 and up

second floor, while no doubt daydreaming about driving out of the store with every toy imaginable. Remember Tom Hanks dancing on the giant floor keyboard in the movie *Big?* Well it's still here, along with today's favorite computer games, video games, and blocks sold by the pound!

With all those toys (and toy operators) creeping, crawling, beeping, and zipping around the store, it's easy to long for the solitude of a sensory-deprivation chamber. But lest you think it's only kids who play with the toys at F.A.O. Schwarz, just take a look around. There are plenty of parents exploring the wizardry of new inventions—ostensibly, so they can try before they buy (uh huh!)—and rediscovering their own childhood in those tried and true toys.

HEY, KIDS! Have you worked up an appetite after all that shopping and playing? Exit the store on the Madison Avenue side to sample the treats at F.A.O. Schweetz. Grab a bag and scoop to your sweet tooth's delight or until your parents say "when." Old favorites like jaw breakers, gummy bears, and licorice share the shelves with the latest in candy cuisine.

FEDERAL HALL NATIONAL MEMORIAL

46

B uilt in 1703 to serve as New York's City Hall, Federal Hall became the first Capitol of the United States under the Constitution and is often considered the birthplace of our nation's government. On its steps stands a statue of George Washington created in 1883 by a relative of his, sculptor John Quincy Adams Ward. Washington was sworn in as the country's first president on that very site in 1789.

The original building was demolished in 1812, and the present structure, occupying the same site, was completed in 1842 and served as a U.S. Customs House. This Greek Revival building was modeled after the Parthenon, another symbol of democracy. As you approach the impressive exterior, notice the 16 Doric columns constructed of Tuckahoe marble, quarried in nearby Westchester County. There are five separate pieces in each column, and each piece weighs 10–12 tons. Walk through the front doors and you pass from Greece to Rome. The rotunda is based on the Pantheon and has 16 Corinthian columns.

HEY, KIDS! Show me the money! When Federal Hall was a customs house (1842–62), millions in gold and silver were stored in basement vaults. No money—only exhibits—remain. Though people think of customs today mainly as a watchdog that prevents smuggling, in colonial times, it collected large fees from merchant vessels. In fact, these fees were so big that they paid for setting up the new U.S. government; creating a navy; planning and building Washington, D.C.; constructing the military academy at West Point; and reducing the national debt to zero in 1835.

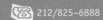

Begin your visit with a 10-minute animated video on the history of majestic Federal Hall, from the trial of Peter Zenger to the inauguration of George Washington. An exhibit on the Zenger trial, a milestone in the establishment of freedom of the press, also includes an antique printing press. Can you imagine printing anything longer than a page on such a primitive press? Other key events that took place in the original building include the Stamp Act Congress of 1765, meetings of the Continental Congress, the enactment of the Northwest Ordinance, the adoption of the Bill of Rights, and the first meeting of the Congress of the United States.

Models of the original structure as City Hall and exhibits about the city and the Wall Street area are interesting, too. Look for historical memorabilia such as the bible used to swear in President Washington. Free guided tours cover the history of the buildings and interpretations of memorabilia and displays. It's like a social studies textbook come to life!

KID-FRIENDLY EATS **Burritoville** (20 John St., tel. 212/766-2020) is a haven for cheap, healthy, and hefty burritos to please every palate. With its number of shops rising like its delicious breads, **Cosi Sandwich Bar** (55 Broad St., tel. 212/344-5000) delights deli lovers with tasty sandwiches—worth the wait. Also *see* South Street Seaport Museum and New York Unearthed.

KEEP IN MIND In addition to finding information at Federal Hall about Federal Hall itself, you can also obtain brochures with self-guided themed walking tours of Lower Manhattan. While you're in the area, check out Castle Clinton, Fraunces Tavern, the Top of the World Trade Center, Ellis Island, the Statue of Liberty, the National Museum of the American Indian (*see* listings for each), and the Staten Island Ferry, just to name a few.

FORBES MAGAZINE GALLERIES

The Forbes Magazine Galleries showcase changing exhibitions from the magazine's collection of paintings, photographs, and autographs, but the big draw for kids is the personal collection of the late publisher Malcolm Forbes, on the ground floor, which includes toys and games and other unusual and sparkling items.

Items in the Toy Galleries include over 500 toy boats and an army of 10,000 toy soldiers engaged in imaginative displays. A special concave viewing window lets children enter the whimsical childhood room depicted in Robert Louis Stevenson's poem, "The Land of Counterpane." Also ongoing here is a display of original handcrafted versions of the board game Monopoly and the game that inspired it: the Landlord's Game. A 1913 English version called the Br'er Fox an' Br'er Rabbit game is also exhibited.

But Forbes's noted collection goes far beyond toys to include historical documents and memorabilia. Thomas Jefferson's bottle of 1787 Château Lafite, Abraham Lincoln's

HEY, KIDS!

Do you collect anything? When did you start? Don't worry if your collection is a little smaller than Forbes's; he had a whole lifetime and a lot of money to spend. To have even more fun, visit the library to learn more about your treasures and how to catalog them.

KEEP IN MIND For children (and adults!) truly smitten by what they see, here are a few publications to check out: *Forbes Galleries* covers collection highlights and has an introduction from the collector himself. *A Lifetime of Collecting* is Forbes's autobiography, containing 572 photographs showcasing many of his treasures. *Toy Boats* offers a pictorial history of the rare tin, cast-iron, and wooden boats, dating from 1870 to 1955, in the Forbes collection.

stovepipe hat, and various presidential papers reveal the personalities and problems of many U.S. presidents. Three miniature rooms—Washington's headquarters at the Battle of Yorktown, John Adams's kitchen law office in Massachusetts, and Jefferson's bedroom and study at Monticello—forge snapshots of American history.

If your youngsters find history dull, they might find the trophies, medals, and awards in the Mortality of Immortality exhibit shinier and more interesting. As Forbes wrote, "the trophy memorabilia are humbling reminders that objects marking great occasions or victories cannot stop the march of time and that, as the pharaohs learned, you can't take the stuff with you." Even more likely to catch the young gallery visitor's eye are 12 of the fabled Easter eggs made by the House of Fabergé for the last two Russia czars, along with over 350 other treasures made under the direction of master jeweler/goldsmith Peter Carl Fabergé. The collection can't help but make you think that, wealth and power notwithstanding, Forbes had a lot of kid in him.

KID-FRIENDLY EATS In the mood for a burger and fries? Try **Elephant and Castle** (68 Greenwich Ave., tel. 212/243–1400). For big, big, big burritos at low, low, low prices, try **Benny's Burritos** (113 Greenwich Ave., tel. 212/727–0584). **NoHo Star** (330 Lafayette St., tel. 212/925–0070) offers American as well as Chinese fare. Children will probably opt for hamburgers and french fries, omelets, or pancakes while parents can be a bit more adventurous.

FRAUNCES TAVERN MUSEUM

The fact that this sight is open on July 4 and Washington's birthday (though closed on other holidays) should immediately tell you who and what are the subjects of this museum. Fraunces Tavern—a large brick house built by Etienne Delancey in 1719 on the city's first landfill—was a meeting place for the Sons of Liberty as well as the site where George Washington said farewell to his loyal officers at the Revolution's end. Today it serves as a museum of early American history and culture, a survivor of the early days of New York City.

The building got its name from tavern-keeper Samuel Fraunces, who ran one the finest dining and drinking establishments in colonial New York. Colonial governor George Clinton threw a huge gala here on Evacuation Day, when the last British soldiers left American soil. The tavern building was also where the Departments of War, State, and Treasury were housed when New York was the first capital of the United States.

KID-FRIENDLY EATS It's more expensive than the neighborhood's many delis, coffee shops, and sandwich places, but if you want to go back in time, dine at the **Fraunces Tavern** (tel. 212/269–0144), part of the complex that includes the museum. It's good for a basic breakfast or for pot roast. (Like many of the area's restaurants catering to a Wall Street crowd, the tavern is closed on weekends.) Also see eateries in the South Street Seaport Museum and New York Unearthed.

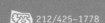
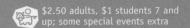

Start at the Visitor Orientation Exhibition, which illustrates the history of the tavern and early New York. From there, visit the Long Room, site of Washington's famous farewell address and now a re-created 18th-century public tavern room. The Clinton Room, named for George Clinton, the first American-born governor of New York, represents an early 19th-century private dining room. A Flash of Color: Early American Flags and Standards highlights national symbols from different periods throughout American history. Included are regimental flags from the Revolution, flags of French troops, and naval banners. Changing exhibitions also shed light on Colonial times.

Summer Sundays welcome you to participate in special events, like tavern games, candle-making, and ice cream socials, for a modest fee. Reservations are recommended. And on those special holidays—Washington's birthday and Independence Day—Fraunces Tavern Museum holds open houses where you may pay as you wish to partake in the day's festivities.

HEY, KIDS! Once a month you can take part in Family Saturday Workshops, de-signed for children of all abilities and free with museum admission. Recent programs have included a history hunt, sailor's arts, Colonial arts and crafts, flag flying, and a spies program, complete with real Revolutionary codes, invisible ink, and quill pens.

KEEP IN MIND Walking tours and Colonial Tea Parties are just some of the public programs held at the Fraunces Tavern Museum that can enrich your museum experience. But it's a good idea to call the museum's recorded informa-tion line ahead of time to determine which of the upcoming programs are ap-propriate for the ages in your family.

HISTORIC RICHMOND TOWN

43

I n the heart of Staten Island, this beautiful 100-acre park may be one of the city's best-kept secrets. The village contains 28 preserved historic buildings and a few reconstructions that interpret three centuries of Staten Island's daily life and culture. Ten buildings are on their original sites; the others were moved from elsewhere on Staten Island.

The village of Richmond began in the 1690s as a crossroads settlement among scattered farms. The Congregation of the Reformed Dutch Church built a combined religious meeting house, school, and residence for its lay minister and teacher around 1695. By 1730, Richmond had become the island's principal political center, and throughout the 18th century, the village continued to increase in importance, acquiring a jail, courthouse, churches, taverns, and shops. By the early 19th century it had become a popular retreat for city residents.

Few barricades separate visitors from the places where people once worked and lived. Each room, whether equipped with the tools of a trade or suffused with the aroma of something

HEY, KIDS!

More than 200 of the best-loved toys from the 1840s through the 1990s are on display in the Historical Museum. Can you recognize what the toys were and how children played with them? Then try to imagine what childhood, family life, and work were like in the days of those toys.

KEEP IN MIND If you're planning a visit, call to see if any special family events (reservations required for some) are coming up. A sampling includes Halloween in Richmond Town, Old Home Day, Christmas in Richmond Town, a Victorian Masquerade Ball, an Independence Day Celebration, Pumpkin Picking at the Decker Farm, a Civil War Encampment Weekend, and a Victorian Valentine Party. The Richmond County Fair also takes place here, combining traditional events with modern pastimes.

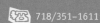 441 Clarke Ave., Staten Island

 718/351-1611

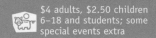 $4 adults, $2.50 children 6–18 and students; some special events extra

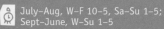 July–Aug, W–F 10–5, Sa–Su 1–5; Sept–June, W–Su 1–5

3 and up

baking, will take you back in time. Begin at the 1837 Third County Courthouse Visitor Center to get a visitor's guide to the 40 points of interest. The Historical Museum is in the former County Clerk's Office. The Voorlezer's House is Richmond's oldest building on its original site as well as the country's oldest elementary schoolhouse. A one-room grocery store from Eltingville now depicts an 1860 printing shop. Your children will chuckle at the outhouse and marvel at demonstrations of printing, tinsmithing, and other trades performed by artisans in period costumes. When demonstrations aren't happening, a guide is present to give an overview of the setting and answer questions.

Special events are offered at various times, but you can count on traditional folk and ethnic music—showcased in the Tavern Concert Series—on Saturday evenings, January–April. The 19th-century Guyon Tavern is warmed by a woodstove and lit by candles to add to the atmosphere.

KID-FRIENDLY EATS **The Parsonage** (74 Arthur Kill Rd., tel. 718/351-7879) serves some history with your meal! It was the official residence of the Reformed Dutch Church minister (1855–1875). **M. Bennett Refreshments** is in the former cellar bakery in the Greek Revival–style Bennett House. The popular summertime traditional dinner, held once a year, includes an Early American menu prepared over open fires with music, games, and century-old toasts (reservations required). A picnic area is just east of the visitor center.

INTREPID SEA AIR SPACE MUSEUM

42

Not your typical museum, the Intrepid Sea Air Space Museum is a unique part of the landscape—make that seascape—of Manhattan's west side. The U.S.S. *Intrepid,* a 40,000-ton, 900-foot-long aircraft carrier, launched in 1943, was once scheduled to be scrapped after 31 years of military service. However, in 1982, after a successful campaign to save it, this historic ship was put into different service—as a museum.

Your children don't have to know history to sense adventure when standing among dozens of vintage and modern aircraft parked wing to wing on the carrier's flight deck, or when hearing a former crew member tell stories of this noble vessel. Video kiosks display the ship's heroic past, which includes five kamikaze strikes, one torpedo attack, and seven bombs. After each repair, the ship returned to active duty, earning her a reputation as the "Ghost Ship."

But there are other craft here, too. You can take a guided tour of the U.S.S. *Edson,* from its impressive engine room to its mess decks. The 418-foot Vietnam-era naval destroyer is the

KID-FRIENDLY EATS When was the last time you dined on a 900-foot-long aircraft carrier? Take the opportunity now, and picnic at tables available for those who bring their own lunch. A variety of sandwiches, snacks, and drinks can also be purchased on board. As you go ashore, head for **Mike's American Bar and Grill** (650 10th Ave., tel. 212/246–4115) for friendly service and fun food without a big bill.

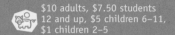
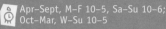
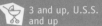
most thoroughly restored vessel here. Don't miss the U.S.S. *Growler,* the only intact strategic missile submarine open to the public. Since 1989, this 3,000-ton, 317-foot-long sub has offered a firsthand look at life on board as well as the once "top-secret" command post. And you can tour the Lockheed A-12 Blackbird, the world's ultimate spy plane. Along with the Blackbird, the *Intrepid*'s aircraft collection includes WWII fighters, supersonic jets, wood and canvas biplanes, and an F-16 Air Force Falcon, just to name a few.

Also here is Felix DeWeldon's original sculpture of the Iwo Jima Memorial, which portrays five marines and a sailor raising a U.S. flag during WWII. (The more famous, larger version is on display at Arlington National Cemetery.) Like the rest of the exhibits at this museum, it's a tribute to the people and vessels who have served our country at sea.

HEY, KIDS! Fly your own jet mission aboard a navy flight simulator in Desert Storm Strike. Take off in your F-18 Hornet jet fighter from the flight deck of an aircraft carrier somewhere in the Persian Gulf. Dodge enemy tanks, missiles, and hostile aircraft as you attempt to return unharmed. Admission to this thrill ride is $5 in addition to your museum entry fee.

KEEP IN MIND Prepare your kids ahead of time that there may be a wait to tour the U.S.S. *Growler.* Access is limited to only 13 people at a time, and very young children are not allowed aboard. And if you have a friend or relative who served or serves aboard ship, you might want to bring him or her along; someone with firsthand experiences can certainly enhance your children's firsthand experience of this museum.

JEWISH MUSEUM

4

Nestled in the elegant 1908 Warburg Mansion, on the city's Museum Mile, the Jewish Museum chronicles 4,000 years of history and culture. The permanent exhibition, called Culture and Continuity, the Jewish Journey, occupies 17 galleries on the third and fourth floors of the museum. You and your family can pick up a free booklet that outlines a self-guided tour through this core exhibit. Art, artifacts, and media installations examine both perpetual and changing aspects of the Jewish cultural experience. Young visitors tend to find the re-creation of an ancient synagogue of interest, whereas older children enjoy television and radio programs from the museum's broadcast archive as well as a film on Jewish rituals in a gallery filled with ceremonial objects.

In addition, many areas and programs at the Jewish Museum are specifically devoted to children. The fourth-floor Children's Gallery has changing exhibitions for young visitors, and each always includes interactive components for inquiring minds and busy hands. On Sunday, you can drop into the Family Activity Center and participate in a hands-on crafts

HEY, KIDS!

If you're a high school junior or senior interested in the arts, check out the Summerarts program (July–August). The four-week session includes studio classes, a behind-the-scenes museum tour, studio visits, and cultural excursions exploring art and contemporary Jewish culture.

KEEP IN MIND If your family finds it hard to come up with something to do on Christmas, consider coming here. Unless December 25 falls on a Saturday, the museum is usually open, and a huge array of family activities is scheduled throughout the day. How many museums do you know of that are open on Christmas?

 1109 5th Ave., at 92nd St.

212/423-3230

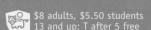 $8 adults, $5.50 students
13 and up; T after 5 free

 Su–M and W–Th 11–5:45, T 11–8; Family
Activity Center Su 1–4; story time Su 1:30

2 and up

workshop for a nominal materials fee; you can also listen to a free ½-hour story time or take part in free Children's Gallery talks, informal interactive minitours of the core exhibit that meet on the third floor. (The museum's first two floors contain temporary exhibits that are more often of interest to adults as well as a gift shop and an orientation video that gives a picture of the building's layout.)

Other family programs include Children's Film Days, in which films are often followed by art workshops related to the movie shown; Stories and Songs for Tots; Art in the Afternoon; and holiday craft and activity workshops. Many events are free; others have a small fee. Family concerts and special performances by well-known artists, like Marc Weiner from *Weinerville,* are scheduled throughout the year. Just check with the museum by phone or at its Web site (www.thejewishmuseum.org) to see if something's happening that would interest your family.

KID-FRIENDLY EATS Lunch, snacks, and a light dinner are available at the museum's **Cafe Weissman.** You can't go wrong at the **Barking Dog Luncheonette** (1678 3rd Ave., tel. 212/831–1800), offering breakfast, lunch, dinner, brunch, and a drinking fountain just for canines, in case you've brought your pooch (though naturally it won't be allowed inside). For home-style, wholesome food, not to mention a great Sunday brunch, try **Sarabeth's** (Hotel Wales, 1295 Madison Ave., tel. 212/410–7335).

JONES BEACH STATE PARK

New York State's most renowned state park opened in 1929 and hosted 1½ million visitors its first year. Sunday traffic jams on the (then) Wantagh Causeway started soon after, and not much has changed since. Today, the Wantagh Parkway still jams up on weekends as families flock to the beach's eight Atlantic Ocean bathing areas and Zachs Bay from points even farther than New York City, 33 miles away.

The park comprises 2,413 acres with 6½ miles of beach frontage and ½ mile of bay frontage. East and West bathhouses also feature Olympic-size pools, diving areas, wading pools, lockers, and showers. A 2-mile boardwalk is popular with young and old, and there are shuffleboard courts, paddle tennis, softball fields, roller-skating, miniature golf, a fitness course, basketball, dancing nightly at the band shell, concerts, and special events.

Surfing is permitted at the West End 2 area from the Monday after Thanksgiving through Labor Day, so surfer-free families may wish to avoid this crowd. With really young children,

HEY, KIDS! As you approach the beach by bus or by car, be on the lookout for the Jones Beach Tower, a familiar landmark modeled after the campanile of St. Mark's Cathedral in Venice. It's 231 feet high and made of brick and stone, housing a 315,000-gallon water tank. Believe it or not, this tower provides all the water for the entire park. So if you're about to ask, "Are we there yet?" just look for the Jones Beach Tower instead.

 Ocean Dr., Wantagh

516/785–1600, 516/221–1000
Jones Beach Theatre

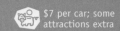 $7 per car; some attractions extra

 Daily sunrise–12 AM

 9 mth and up

head to Zachs Bay, a gentle bathing area (don't even think about waves). Moms and dads have been dutifully depositing tots 10 yards from the family blanket in a puddle of water for years, and it's still a great first ocean experience.

The Jones Beach Theatre, at Zachs Bay, offers a sensational summer concert schedule with seating for 11,200. A 104-foot-wide stage with a 76-foot revolving center has an underwater tunnel leading from shore to stage and underground elevators for supplies and scenery. Though most shows are geared for adult and teenage audiences, some concerts will interest families with youngsters.

The West End area features many undeveloped areas that are home to migratory birds and natural plants. With miles of surf fishing areas, docks, a boat basin, and bait station, Jones Beach is an ideal spot to cast your line as well as to play, sunbathe, and swim. Too bad so many people know it!

TRANSPORTATION By train, take the Long Island Railroad to Freeport or Wantagh, where buses (tel. 212/526–0900) connect to the beach. Bus service also runs from Manhattan via Recreations Lines (tel. 718/788–8000). By car, take the Northern State Parkway, Long Island Expressway, or Southern State Parkway east to the Meadowbrook or Wantagh parkways south to the park.

KID-FRIENDLY EATS Part of the fun of the beach is crunching that sand in your peanut butter sandwich. But for those who choose not to cart a 10-ton cooler across the beach, refreshment stands dispense drinks, cool desserts, hot dogs, and snacks. Barbecue and picnic areas are also abundant. The **Board-walk Restaurant and Terrace** (Central Mall, tel. 516/785–2840) features lunch, dinner, and Sunday Brunch. The **Seaside Sweet Shoppe** (West Bath-house), modeled on an old-fashioned ice-cream parlor, has table and counter service.

LIBERTY SCIENCE CENTER

Many consider this one of the nation's top 10 science centers. The first thing to wow your children (and you) is the 700-pound Hoberman Sphere, which expands and contracts repeatedly in the atrium. It's mesmerizing to watch it seemingly explode into the huge space. But don't linger too long, or you'll miss all the fun on the three theme floors.

On the Environment Floor, you can climb across a 20-foot rock wall full of fossils or take a close look at sea urchins and spider crabs in the Touch Tank. Get your hands dirty at the Stream Table before making friends with insects, snakes, and reptiles in the Green House Discovery Room.

A popular Health Floor destination for the 7-and-up crowd is the Touch Tunnel. Crawl through this 100-foot black tube with only your sense of touch to guide you. Close by is the Perception Maze, where you can enter the world of optical illusion. At the medical imaging station, you can use state-of-the-art MRI and CT scans to explore the human body.

HEY, KIDS!

You can visit the science center's Web site at www.lsc.org, where you'll meet Betty Bug—a.k.a. Dr. Betty Faber, staff scientist and entomologist, who will show you some cool stuff to see and do. It's the "creepiest" Web site you'll ever log onto.

KID-FRIENDLY EATS Check out the **Laser Lights Cafe,** on the main floor, for reasonably priced entrées that appeal to both young and old. Choose from pizza, burgers and fries, franks, chili with cheese, sandwiches, and salads. This cafeteria makes for a nice break in a full day and a good place to plan your strategy for the afternoon.

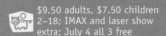
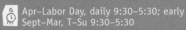
Next comes the Invention Floor. At the Chromakey stage, use the magic of video to put people on the moon or in a jungle. Challenge a computer in the virtual sports stadium to basketball, Ping-Pong, or soccer. At the USAF Flight Simulator, navigate a plane over a 100-mile radius from the science center, passing many New York landmarks.

Each exhibit floor has a discovery room, where staff present hands-on activities, and a science demonstration stage, where informative and entertaining shows take place. Don't miss a 3-D laser journey in the Joseph D. Williams Science Theater or the latest IMAX film on the IMAX Dome Theater's six-story screen. Many of the over 250 participatory exhibits may be too complex for preschoolers, but each floor has some activities for them. Since its 1993 opening, over 5 million visitors have come to Liberty Science Center. Is it any wonder?

TRANSPORTATION Don't let the New Jersey location keep you from making the trip; driving takes under 30 minutes. If you're coming by car, get to New Jersey Turnpike exit 14B, bear left after the tollbooth, and follow signs. Or take the PATH train to Exchange Place in Jersey City or the NY Waterway ferry (see below) from the World Financial Center to Jersey City's Colgate Center, where buses regularly leave for the science center; for bus schedules call 201/432–8048.

LOWER EAST SIDE TENEMENT MUSEUM

38

Chronicling a variety of immigrant and migrant experiences in Manhattan's Lower East Side, this urban living-history experience comprises a series of tours of an 1863 tenement building (the first tenement declared a National Historic Landmark) and its neighborhood. Tours start at the visitor center, where you'll also find a 6-foot model of the tenement filled with furniture and figures representing 12 families who lived there between 1870 and 1915. A free slide show tells the history of the building and neighborhood, and a video features interviews with residents past and present. A gallery hosts changing displays.

There are three guided tours. "Walk the Streets Where We Lived" is a one-hour stroll through the Lower East Side, including public spaces and historic buildings, such as the old Jewish Daily Forward Building on East Broadway. This tour is probably too much for young children. A better choice is the 45-minute "Confino Family Apartment" tour, which focuses on the Sephardic-Jewish Confino family in 1916. "Tour a 19th Century Tenement" is a 45-minute visit to the apartments of the Gumpertz family from Germany, the Rogarshevsky family of

HEY, KIDS! The 45-minute tour of the Confino family's apartment is specially designed as a hands-on experience. You will be met by a costumed guide, who will welcome you as if you are an immigrant just arrived in the neighborhood. Try on period clothing. Ask Mom and Dad to show you how to fox trot to the music on the authentic wind-up Victrola. If you try hard enough, you just might be able to imagine a child's life here in 1916.

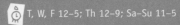 Visitor center, 90 Orchard St., at Broome St.; tenement, 97 Orchard St.

212/431-0233

 1 tour $8 adults, $6 students; additional tours $6 adults, $4 students

 T, W, F 12–5; Th 12–9; Sa–Su 11–5

8–16

Lithuania, and the Baldizzi family from Italy. A look at an unrestored apartment is also part of this tour, as is a holiday season glimpse of the Gumpertz and Baldizzi families' observance of Hanukkah and Christmas. Round-table discussions on mostly adult topics are scheduled year-round as are children's and family programs. The Tenement Theatre at John Schneider's Saloon, in the tenement's basement, stages plays and vaudeville acts relating to Lower East Side history.

If you have a relative or friend who was an immigrant on the Lower East Side, or who knows stories of those days, you might want to invite that person along to provide a first- or second-hand perspective. For a decidedly more modern source of information, take a virtual tour of the museum by logging onto the Channel 13 (WNET) Web site at www.wnet.org/tenement. However you visit, your children will probably gain an appreciation for New York's present by catching a glimpse of its past.

KID-FRIENDLY EATS You can choose food from several different ethnic groups. Have a knish or potato latkes (pancakes) at **Yonah Schimmel's Knoshery** (137 E. Houston St., tel. 212/477–2858), a Lower East Side institution that began from a pushcart a century ago. For dim sum, wonton soup, or veggie dumplings, try **20 Mott Street** (20 Mott St., tel. 212/964–0380).

KEEP IN MIND Tickets for all tours are available at the visitor center on a first-come, first-served basis, and they sell out quickly, as groups are limited to 15. In addition, tickets for weekday tours and programs may be purchased in advance by credit card. Sundays at the museum are especially crowded, but if you come by car, you can enjoy four hours of free parking at a lot on Broome Street, between Norfolk and Suffolk streets, courtesy of the Historic Orchard Street Shopping District.

MADISON SQUARE GARDEN

37

S itting on top of Penn Station, this is perhaps the world's most famous arena. Generations of New Yorkers can fondly remember coming to various incarnations of "the Garden" to see a variety of sports, from boxing to basketball, as well as other types of performances. Today's Madison Square Garden traces its beginnings to the 1874 Great Roman Hippodrome, built by showman P.T. Barnum. In 1877 it was taken over by bandmaster Patrick Gilmore and renamed Gilmore's Garden. In 1879 Cornelius Vanderbilt's son William renamed the complex Madison Square Garden, and so its descendent is known today.

The main arena seats 20,000 and is the spring site of performances by Ringling Bros. and Barnum & Bailey Circus. It is also home to the New York Knicks basketball team and the New York Rangers hockey team, as well as events ranging from tennis tournaments to boxing bouts and from horse shows to track meets. In 1877 Gilmore's Garden played host to the first annual N.Y. Bench Show, now famous as the Westminster Kennel Club Dog Show. Various ice shows and other children's fare are offered throughout the year. The 5,600-seat Paramount

HEY, KIDS!

The Walk of Fame showcases names—from Elton John to Billie Jean King to Gunther Gebel-Williams—representing over a century of memorable sports and entertainment. In 1992 the first 25 members, chosen from over 240 nominees, were inducted. See how many famous people you can identify.

KID-FRIENDLY EATS There are many restaurants on the lower concourse of Pennsylvania Station, or get a deli sandwich at **Ben's Kosher Delicatessen** (209 W. 38th St., tel. 212/398-2367). Having a snack attack? Dunk a donut at **Krispy Kreme** (2 Penn Plaza, 33rd St. on Amtrak level, tel. 212/947-7175). Head to Macy's Herald Square and **Emack & Bolio's** (151 W. 34th St., 4th floor, tel. 212/494-5853) for creamy, rich ice cream and yogurt in flavors you can only dream about.

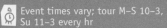

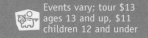 7th Ave. between 31st and 33rd Sts.

 212/465-6000 box office;
212/465-5800 tours

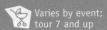 Events vary; tour $13
ages 13 and up, $11
children 12 and under

Event times vary; tour M–S 10–3,
Su 11–3 every hr

Varies by event;
tour 7 and up

Theater, today known as the Theater at Madison Square Garden, also hosts children's shows, such as *Sesame Street Live, The Wizard of Oz,* and *A Christmas Carol.*

In addition to attending an event at the Garden, your family can take a one-hour Behind the Scenes Tour, which starts in the box office lobby under the distinctive Bulova Clock and continues through the arena, the theater, the luxurious Garden suites, the historic Walk of Fame, and the locker rooms of the Knicks and Rangers. The tour is an exciting add-on if you're planning to attend a sporting event here, especially if your children are true sports fans.

TRANSPORTATION It's "easy" to drive here, but beware of traffic. By subway, take the 1, 2, 3, or 9 (7th Avenue line) or the A, C, or E (8th Avenue line) to Penn Station or the B, D, F, N, Q, R, or PATH trains to 34th Street and 6th Avenue. The LIRR, NJ Transit, and Amtrak all stop in Penn Station. From Grand Central, take the subway shuttle to Times Square and then a 7th Avenue subway. By bus, take the M4 or M10 here or any north–south bus to 34th Street and transfer to the M34 or M16 crosstown.

METROPOLITAN MUSEUM OF ART

At 2 million square feet, the Met, as it's known, is the largest art museum in the Western Hemisphere. Its permanent collection houses nearly 3 million works of art from all over the world, including objects from the Paleolithic era to modern times. While you might be afraid that this immense museum will overwhelm your little ones, rest assured that it won't if you explore no more than two to four sections of it on any given visit. Free lectures and walking tours covering various parts of the museum are informative for older students—though not necessarily slower-moving, fidgety youngsters—and self-guided audio tours are also available. But whatever the age of your children and however you choose to explore the Met, do explore it. It's truly one of the city's best sights.

Certain areas of the Met are particularly fascinating to children, and yours will no doubt enjoy the Costume Institute on the ground floor as well as the musical instruments on the second floor by the American Wing's courtyard. Check out the collectors' baseball cards in the first-floor American Wing side gallery. And when it's time to take a break, relax on the benches

HEY, KIDS! Want to go on a treasure hunt? Just ask at the information desk for "Family Gallery Guides" and "Museum Hunts." Be sure to visit the popular Arms and Armor Hall. What do you think it's like to wear a suit of armor? How heavy do you think it is? Also visit the Egyptian Galleries. Check out the mummies and the Temple of Dendur, a real Egyptian temple moved here to save it from destruction after the Aswan High Dam was built.

in the courtyard of the American Wing, and admire the plantings and statues of a Native American and of a mountain lion and her family. In the Asian galleries, the Astor Court Chinese garden showcases a Ming Dynasty scholar's courtyard, complete with water splashing over artfully placed stones.

On Friday and Saturday nights, the Great Hall Balcony Quintet plays on the second-floor balcony. Sit close on the benches across from the musicians so your kids can watch. After a little night music, explore the nearby galleries. At 6 or 7:30, you can attend a free one-hour family lecture and sketching workshop for kids 6–12 and an adult companion. Free Saturday family programs and a family film series round out the special events for kids here. If you start slowly and with age-appropriate activities, your children can enjoy a lifetime of discovering this museum.

KID-FRIENDLY EATS Eat in the **Museum Café** (tel. 212/570–3964), or have a burger and fries at **Luke's Bar and Grill** (1396 3rd Ave., tel. 212/249–7070). Since 1925, the **Lexington Candy Shop** (1226 Lexington Ave., tel. 212/288–0057) has been serving milkshakes and malteds, cheeseburgers and crinkle fries to the luncheonette crowd. It's worth a trip back in time.

KEEP IN MIND The gift shop stocks unusual kids' toys, games, and books, so it's a good source for birthday gifts that children won't already have. One of the sweetest and most pertinent purchases here is the musical video *Don't Eat the Pictures: Sesame Street at the Metropolitan Museum of Art.* Starring Big Bird, Cookie Monster (at whom the title admonition is directed), and the rest of the gang, it's a great introduction to the museum for youngsters. Better yet, get a copy before you visit, so your children will feel in the know before they go.

MUSEUM OF AMERICAN FOLK ART

There's something about folk art that appeals to children. Perhaps it's the seeming simplicity, the depictions of everyday objects and creatures, or the frequent flights of whimsy. But whatever the reason, your children will probably enjoy this collection of artworks from the 18th, 19th, and 20th centuries. The museum is primarily divided into the Daniel Cowin Permanent Collection Gallery and two changing exhibit spaces. The permanent collection highlights America's folk art heritage through paintings, sculpture, furniture, textiles, and decorative arts. Temporary exhibits can spotlight a particular artist or theme, such as religious folk art, patriotic folk art, or work from a particular region, such as New England.

Some of the items worth seeing are the dolls, painted wood carousel horses, weather vanes, and whirligigs. *Uncle Sam Riding a Bicycle,* a sculpture that moves in the wind, and the colorful turn-of-the-century *Flag Quilt* by Mary Baxter are just two examples of the patriotic art preserved here. You can't miss the 9-foot-high weather vane in the museum's center. The shot marks can still be seen on this decorative "target," which once stood atop a building in East

KID-FRIENDLY EATS Fiorello's Roman Cafe (1900 Broadway, tel. 212/595–5330) serves up minipizzas and, in good weather, outdoor dining. Close to Lincoln Center, the **Saloon** (1920 Broadway, tel. 212/874–1500) has an extensive menu and an occasional skating waiter.

HEY, KIDS! Are you looking for an unusual souvenir, a gift for a friend or family member, or something cool to bring to show-and-tell? The museum shop is a treasure trove of objects handmade by more than 200 American craftspeople in the folk tradition. Or let what you see—like a "beaded" necklace made of tightly wound and shellacked strips of wrapping paper and Sunday comics—inspire you to make your own folk art presents that anyone would be happy to receive.

2 Lincoln Sq., Columbus Ave. and 66th St.

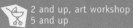 T–Su 11:30–7:30

 212/595–9533

 Free; art workshop $1

2 and up, art workshop 5 and up

Branch, New York. This figure of a legendary Indian chief of the Delaware tribe, known for his eloquence and courage, became a symbol for American soldiers going into battle, and he became known as St. Tammany.

Guided tours, workshops, puppet shows, concerts, and storytelling for families take place year-round. Programs are designed in conjunction with current exhibitions. Afternoon storytelling programs feature authors and artists of popular children's books, who read their work and show their illustrations. Book signings often follow these presentations.

Sunday afternoon art workshops (reservations required) are designed to follow specially guided tours of the museum for children and their families. Projects often complement either a temporary exhibit or an aspect of the permanent collection. Popular past programs have included self-portraits as animals, sock and kitchen-towel people, 3-D comics, and hearts and hands valentines. Your children can join right in.

KEEP IN MIND This urban museum is unique not only in the rich folk heritage of the collection it shares with the public, but also in its free admission—unusual for New York City—and its six-day-a-week evening hours. Its convenient location directly across from Lincoln Center makes it a great spot for a pre-performance museum outing or for one last cultural adventure after you've made a day of the city.

MUSEUM OF THE CITY OF NEW YORK

Where in the world can you find seats from the original Yankee Stadium, a section of the B-25 bomber that crashed into the Empire State Building, a piece of the old mechanical Times Square news "zipper," or the giant bolt tightener used to build the Brooklyn Bridge? At the Museum of the City of New York, of course! For 75 years this museum has gathered together the single most important collection of artifacts related to the history of Gotham. Today it houses over 1.5 million items, including over 2,000 paintings depicting the changing cityscape as well as 500,000 photographs documenting city history.

Start by viewing the "Big Apple Video," shown every ½ hour. This 22-minute documentary tells the city's story through paintings, prints, photos, film clips, and other artifacts from the museum's extensive collections. In the Fire Gallery, your children can learn of the earliest bucket brigades and see the hose carriage and pumpers that were pulled not by horses, but by the firefighters. Check out the collection of city vehicles, including an omnibus, ambulance, police paddy wagon, and a Checker Cab.

HEY, KIDS! For an overview, check out the museum's Web site—www.mcny.org. Go to the area called Museum Collections Sampler to take an in-depth look at the exhibitions and collections featured, including pictures and information. The site also includes some items and exhibitions only seen on the Web, including New Foot Notes, a collection of 18th-century women's shoes from the costume collection. Also check out the 19th-century New York City valentine. Updated daily, this research tool also contains a calendar of family events.

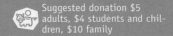

Your youngsters will be fascinated with the toy collection in the New York Toy Stories gallery space, which features more than 26,000 toys dating from Colonial times to the present, including over 1,000 antique dolls, 300 children's games, and an unusual collection of furnished dollhouses dating from 1769 to the 1970s. Your kids can also visit the museum's collection of marine-related artifacts, including ship models, ships' figureheads, and paintings. The precious metals collection, ranked one of the eight finest public holdings in the country, features thousands of pieces of household and ceremonial silver and gold pieces dating from 1678 to 1984.

Like most good museums these days, this one is home to special exhibitions as well as walking tours, lectures, performances, readings, and family workshops open to the public. Unlike other museums, however, this one has as its subject the very city that it calls home.

KID-FRIENDLY EATS Have a burger at **Peter's Burger Place** (1413 Madison Ave., tel. 212/722–4400). If you're more in the mood to make your own salad, get some soup, or grab a sandwich, head for **Shin's** (1414 Madison Ave., tel. 212/831–1754), a deli-takeout joint with tables in a large room in the back.

KEEP IN MIND Like the city it chronicles, this museum and its four floors of exhibit space are simply too big to see in one visit. Grab a floor plan at the outset of your adventure, and take a vote on what to visit. While the impressive collection of Currier & Ives hand-colored lithographs and drawings may not be your kids' idea of fun (although you never know), the theater collection, which includes 3,500 costumes and the personal collections of well-known Broadway performers, might leave them star- and stagestruck.

MUSEUM OF MODERN ART

Nicknamed MoMA, this museum maintains the world's foremost collection of 20th-century art: over 100,000 paintings, sculptures, drawings, prints, photographs, architectural models and drawings, and design objects. But the museum also offers programs for toddlers to teens that encourage parents and kids to learn about modern art together.

The core of MoMA's permanent collection is displayed on the second and third floors. Second-floor galleries include Postimpressionism, cubism, surrealism, and Mexican art of the 1930s; rotating photography exhibits are also here. The third floor focuses on abstract expressionism, pop art (most kids think it's fun), and contemporary works. Drawings, prints, and illustrated books are on the third floor; architecture and design on the fourth.

Most children's programs take place on Saturdays. Tours for Tots offers 45-minute gallery activities that introduce 4-year-olds to painting and sculpture. In Two-in-a-Row, a one-hour program on two consecutive weeks, school-age children learn to look at and talk about art

HEY, KIDS! Log onto the museum's Art Safari Web subsite (www.moma.org/online-projects/artsafari) to take part in a project based on the book of the same name. Using animation, sound, and visuals, the subsite teaches you about the artworks covered in the book, invites you to create art based on what you've learned, and then poses some questions to get you writing. You can even submit your artwork or writing and have it displayed online—almost like a worldwide museum.

11 W. 53rd St.; Edward John Noble
Education Center, 18 W. 54th St.

 Th and Sa–T 10:30–6, F 10:30–8:30

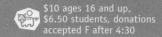 $10 ages 16 and up,
$6.50 students, donations
accepted F after 4:30

212/708-9400

 4 and up

in the museum's galleries. Both programs are held at MoMA's Edward John Noble Education Center, and preregistration is required. The one-hour One-at-a-Time includes guided walks through the galleries on such topics as Make Me Laugh, Humor in Art and Seeing in the Dark. No pre-registration is required, and sign-in begins at 9:45 at the education center.

As part of the one-hour Family Films, shown in the Titus Theater 2, classic film shorts may include live action and animation and may range from documentary to fantasy. A museum educator introduces the films, directs discussion, and provides follow-up activities for gallery visits. Tickets are available at the lobby information desk. Two-hour family art workshops on varying topics are also offered Saturday, as are free classes and films for high-school students. Saturdays are certainly chock-full, but no matter when you visit, your family will have a rich, distinctly modern experience here.

KID-FRIENDLY EATS The museum's **Garden Café** and **Sette Moma** (tel. 212/708–9710) are convenient places to grab a bite. The former is more kid-friendly, offering sandwiches, fruit, snacks, salads, and drinks, whereas the latter serves full sit-down Italian meals. Also see Radio City Music Hall, Rockefeller Center and the Ice Rink, and Sony Wonder Technology Lab.

KEEP IN MIND Art Safari: An Adventure in Looking takes you on a search for animals, specifically those in eight important works. Families are invited to ask questions, talk, and explore art. The book even offers learning-extension activities to do at home. An Art Safari family package ($11.50) includes museum admission for one adult and up to four children 5–12 and a copy of the book.

MUSEUM OF TELEVISION AND RADIO

It's not hard to imagine what the attraction of this museum is, for students of radio and TV and families alike. The broadcast collection comprises over 100,000 TV and radio programs and commercial tapes from the 1920s to the present, and three galleries contain photographs and artifacts that tell the history of broadcasting. Your family can even view radio and television scripts on microfiche or watch TV for two hours at a time at any of 96 consoles throughout the museum. Catch classic Jack Benny or early Ed Sullivan shows, watch the first moon walk, Uncle Milty, *I Love Lucy* reruns, or the Beatles' first appearance on American television. Other facilities here include four theaters and a radio-listening room, where you can drop in on TV and radio shows. Pick up a daily schedule at the front desk.

Recent special temporary exhibits have included a display of masks and costumes from *Star Trek,* with a peek behind the makeup of this very popular program, as well as Sesame Street's Art from the Fuzzy and the Famous, an exhibit of personal art from celebrity guests on the program, cast members, puppeteers, and special friends of the show, all compiled in

HEY, KIDS!

If you're 8–13 and want to be on the radio, come for a Saturday radio workshop. No, you won't be the guest DJ on your favorite radio station—nothing that glamorous! Instead you can try re-creating performances and sound effects from shows of the '30s and '40s.

KEEP IN MIND

If you'd like to watch vintage television footage or commercials, get to the museum early. Go to the library, and search a computer database for the program you want to view. Then sign up for a time at an assigned console on the third or fifth floor. At the appointed hour, your program "pops up" on your console, which is equipped with headphones. Many consoles can accommodate more than one viewer, so you can watch with other family members. If the consoles are taken, head to the fifth-floor radio listening room or survey what's running in the small, comfortable theaters.

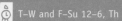
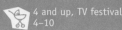
celebration of the program's 30th anniversary. There's always something new in the temporary gallery spaces, with regular visitors returning frequently to check out the latest special screenings or exhibits.

The International Children's Television Festival, running from late November through mid-December, provides an opportunity to see the best of children's television from around the world at weekend afternoon screenings. Also included in this popular festival are interactive workshops with an international flavor, focusing on music, storytelling, and puppetry.

Frequently throughout the year, live radio broadcasts take place at the museum's on-site studio. Morning drive time, music, talk shows, and book chats are just some of the formats that can be heard during these programs. These broadcasts are open to the public, and children will be able to see what happens behind the scenes of a radio show.

KID-FRIENDLY EATS For a meal on a bun, visit **Burger Heaven** (20 E. 49th St., tel. 212/755–2166; 536 Madison Ave., tel. 212/753–4214; 9 E. 53rd St., tel. 212/752–0240). For a simulated space flight, visit **Mars 2112** (1633 Broadway, tel. 212/582–2112). Have your cameras ready for Martians, while you eat a full-moon pizza, crater burger, solar-flare chicken fingers, or a deep-space freeze before returning to Earth. Also *see* Radio City Music Hall and Rockefeller Center and the Ice Rink.

NATIONAL MUSEUM OF THE
AMERICAN INDIAN

Adults find both the interior and exterior architecture of this museum as interesting as its collection of Native American artifacts. Children tend to be more intrigued by the elaborate feathers, weavings and blankets, baskets, gold work, jade, Aztec mosaics, painted hides, Native American garments, and stone, wood, and horn carvings on display. But whatever your family's interests, you'll find plenty to see and do at this first museum of its kind dedicated to Native American culture.

In 1903, New Yorker George Gustav Heye began gathering a collection of 1 million Indian artifacts from North, Central, and South America. Eventually, it became New York's Museum of the American Indian, with Heye as director, but by late in the century it came under the Smithsonian umbrella, with the stipulation that it remain in New York. Ultimately, the National Museum of the American Indian will also include a research and conservation facility in Suitland, Maryland, and a museum on the National Mall in Washington, D.C., but for now the museum is found only in this New York center named for Heye.

KID–FRIENDLY EATS Try tasty, tempting **Daily Soup** (55 Broad St., tel. 212/269–2336), a celebrity hangout with a great modestly priced breakfast, brunch, and lunch. At **Bubby's** (120 Hudson St., tel. 212/219–0666), eat sandwiches, fish, or breakfast to late afternoon.

KEEP IN MIND The museum offers two kids' programs that are fascinating, fun, and free. The annual *Harvest Ceremony: Beyond the Thanksgiving Myth* is an interactive theater piece offering a fresh historical perspective on the first Thanksgiving and usually performed in November for National American Indian Heritage Month. In May, a weekend afternoon Children's Festival has plays, storytelling, crafts, dance, films, museum talks, and hands-on learning activities. Information regarding these and other activities can be found on the NMAI Web site: www.si.edu/nmai.

The center occupies the first two floors of the Alexander Hamilton U.S. Custom House, a beautiful Beaux Arts–style building that is both a National Historic Landmark and a New York City Landmark. Outside are 44 columns, each adorned with the head of Mercury, the Roman god of commerce. Inside in the rotunda, a 140-ton skylit dome appears to soar overhead without any visible means of support. The symmetry of the Great Hall is complemented by monumental arches and columns.

The museum's collection spans more than 10,000 years of Indian heritage and includes cultural, historical, and artistic artifacts as well as items of spiritual significance. It's interesting to note that religious and cultural items are on display only with the approval of the appropriate tribes. Educational enrichment programs and presentations on living cultures are offered throughout the year. Call ahead to see if any special programs are scheduled for the day of your visit.

HEY, KIDS! Outside the building's huge entrance are four large sculptures, representing America, Asia, Europe, and Africa. The America statue features a Native American figure peering out from behind a throne. He wears a feather headdress and is surrounded by a totem pole and broken southwestern pottery. In 1907, when this customhouse was built, that Indian figure was meant to symbolize the vanishing Native American. Isn't it ironic that in the 1990s this site became a museum dedicated to Native American life?

NBC STUDIOS BACKSTAGE TOUR

It's not a sure bet that you'll see any television stars, but you never know whom you may bump into in the halls of 30 Rockefeller Plaza when you take the NBC studio tour. But that shouldn't be the main reason for your family to take this one-hour tour. The real reason to go behind the scenes is to learn some of the fascinating secrets of television production as well as some of the history of TV in general and the National Broadcasting Company in particular.

NBC has been offering tours since 1933. An NBC page serves as your guide through the world of the peacock network. And who knows? Your page may go on to become famous, like some other former pages: Ted Koppel, Willard Scott, Regis Philbin, Steve Allen, Kate Jackson, and Michael Eisner.

Along your journey, you'll go back in time to NBC's birth in the Golden Age of Radio. Then you'll fast-forward to a time before fast-forward buttons, through many landmark TV programs

HEY, KIDS! Want to attend a live taping of a TV show? *The Rosie O'Donnell Show* tapes Monday through Thursday here. Just ask a parent to write or call for information. You must be at least 5 to attend a taping—lower than the minimum ages of 6 for the tour and 16 to see *Saturday Night Live* live. Stand-by tickets are distributed at 7:30 the day of the show, outside on the 49th Street side of the building.

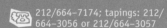

that your grandparents and parents used to watch. You'll walk your way to the present, through various current studios, probably for two or three of the following programs: *Saturday Night Live, NBC Nightly News, Late Night with Conan O'Brien, Today,* and *Dateline NBC.* You'll also learn about the latest TV technology used to broadcast around the world. Visitors can see themselves on TV in a ministudio, where one lucky tour-taker will do the weather. Because of fast-breaking news events and changes in broadcast schedules, this unstaged tour varies from day to day.

A small NBC museum is now part of a retail attraction titled the NBC Experience, located directly across from *Today'*s Studio 1A, on the corner of 49th Street and Rockefeller Plaza. The museum features memorabilia from NBC's long history—items like the first Howdy Doody test pattern, a microphone from early radio, a bottle from the original *I Dream of Jeannie,* and tons of photos.

KEEP IN MIND

Individual tickets can now be reserved and purchased in advance by phone with a credit card, as can tickets for groups of 10. (The group rate is $8.50 per person.) Because so many groups book ahead of time, if you do choose to purchase your tickets on the day of your tour, you'll want to get here early. Tours are often sold out by early afternoon.

KID-FRIENDLY EATS At the **American Festival Cafe** (*see* Rockefeller Center and the Ice Rink), ask for a seat overlooking the skating rink in winter, the garden in spring and summer. Pre-theater dinners are a family bargain. Fans like **Mickey Mantle's** (42 Central Park S, tel. 212/688–7777) for its burgers, fried chicken fingers, chicken pot pie, and other large-portion items. Friendly service, oversize TV screens, and memorabilia also hit a home run.

NEW VICTORY THEATER

Surprising as it sounds, this is Manhattan's first theater especially for families and kids. Its year-round season of professional productions by national and international artists is offered at surprisingly affordable ticket prices. Reopened in 1995 as part of the theater district redevelopment, the New Victory was built in 1900 by Oscar Hammerstein and is New York's oldest active theater.

In 1902 impresario David Belasco took over the theater. Dramatic and vaudeville shows continued until 1932, when Billy Minsky opened Broadway's first burlesque in this theater. Next it was renamed the Victory, in the patriotic spirit of WWII, and ran second-run films for several decades. In the 1970s it became the block's first XXX-rated movie house. It seems emblematic of the whole Times Square face-lift that from these cultural ashes has risen a phoenix for families.

The renovation began in 1994, restoring the striking facade of the building with its monumental second-floor entry staircase and globed standing lights. Inside, the opulent

HEY, KIDS!

If you want to learn to juggle or dance or develop another theatrical skill, come to a free pre-performance workshop conducted by professional performers and guest artists and available to members. Each workshop highlights an activity related to the day's performance.

KEEP IN MIND

The New Victory is wheelchair accessible, and wheelchair seats must be purchased in advance. In addition, some performances are sign-language interpreted. Booster seats for small children are also available. The benefits of membership include 40% discounts on ticket prices, priority seating (tickets available to members before they go on sale to the general public), a member-friendly exchange policy, newsletters, various contests, and coupons for local restaurants, parking garages, stores, and other fun activities.

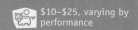

domed auditorium looks almost as it did in the days of the Belasco Theater. Around the rim of the regal central dome are eight plump pairs of golden cherubs, whose feet dangle over the seats below. Adding to the elegant interior are tiers of box seats capped by golden domes. The two-balcony auditorium now holds 500 seats.

Cutting-edge family entertainment from around the globe featuring masters of music, dance, drama, puppetry, and circus arts illuminate the stage at the "New Vic." Recent performances have include the New Shanghai Circus, Grimm Tales, the Doug Elkins Dance Company, and Flamenco Vivo. Performance times vary with each event, running from just under an hour to two hours. Shows can run for as little as three days or as long as three to four weeks.

KID-FRIENDLY EATS Try lunch, brunch, or dinner at **Zuni** (598 9th Ave., tel. 212/765–7626) for reasonable prices and southwestern flavors with Asian and Italian flair. You can't go wrong at **John's Pizza** (260 W. 44th St., tel. 212/391–7560). Also see restaurants in Broadway on a Budget.

NEW YORK AQUARIUM

B y the sea, by the sea, by the beautiful sea . . ." That little ditty conjures up images of crowded old seaside attractions like Coney Island. Alongside the cotton candy and amusements, however, is this aquarium, which first welcomed visitors in 1896 at its former site in Manhattan's Battery Park and moved to this 14-acre location in 1957. It's home to over 10,000 species of marine life, including beluga whales, giant sea turtles, sand-tiger sharks, and sea otters.

Don't miss the dolphin and sea lion demonstrations in the 1,600-seat Aquatheater, but don't sit too close either, unless you're prepared to get splashed. Get touchy-feely with a cow-nosed ray in the touch tank (May–October). Marvel at the re-creation of a rocky Pacific coast habitat for the aquarium's black-footed penguins; harbor, gray, and fur seals; sea otters; and Pacific walruses. Watch them from below water inside or from above water around rocks, trees, and pools outside. Check out the state-of-the-art wave machines, and try to attend one of the feedings throughout the day.

HEY, KIDS! Take a "get wet" workshop, and prepare for oceans of fun. From toddlers to teens, kids share the magic and mystery of the marine world through art, music, science, beach walks, lectures, tours, and other adventures. Free public events also are scheduled, ranging from a '50s dolphin doo-wop party to the Halloween Sea Monsters program. Or dive right in and spend the summer as a Marine Explorer or Junior Oceanographer. Whatever the program, it's sure to be exciting and educational.

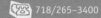 Boardwalk at W. 8th St.,
Coney Island, Brooklyn

718/265-3400

$8.75 ages 14 and up,
$4.50 children 2–13

 Memorial Day–Labor Day, M–F 10–5, Sa–
Su 10–6; early Sept-late May, daily 10–5

All ages

In Discovery Cove, your family can stand under a 400-gallon tidal wave that crashes every 30 seconds. A Plexiglas hood keeps you dry, but the power of the sea may leave you breathless. Hands-on exhibits, interactive videos, games, and marine tanks teach about the ecology of the oceans and marshlands.

The Native Sea Life Exhibit houses an authentic shipwreck as well as the diverse aquatic life found in local waters. Come within inches of 9-foot sharks patrolling the famous safe from the *Andrea Doria,* an Italian cruise ship that sank near Massachusetts in 1956. The safe was sent to the aquarium in 1981 for "safe-keeping." (It's empty now, but when Geraldo Rivera opened it in 1985, it contained a little money.) The Hudson River Exhibit relates the vital waterway's history and includes freshwater and marine habitats featuring sea turtles and moray eels. By the end of your visit, you might just be humming the rest of that ditty: "We'll have fun, we'll have fun, oh how happy we'll be!"

KID-FRIENDLY EATS Pack a lunch and pick a table on the Oceanic Deck or near Discovery Cove. There's an outdoor **snack bar** and an indoor **cafeteria**. **Gargiulo's** (2911 W. 15th St., tel. 718/266–4891) has good Italian food and boisterous crowds, or try **Totonno Pizzeria Napolitano** (1524 Neptune Ave., tel. 718/372–8606). The boardwalk has fast food.

KEEP IN MIND A family membership in the Wildlife Conservation Society costs only $58 and lets everyone in your family visit the aquarium, the Bronx Zoo, the Central Park Wildlife Center, the Prospect Park Wildlife Center, *and* the Queens Wildlife Center free for a year. Quite the bargain! You also get a year's subscription to *Wildlife Conservation Magazine*, a great read and valuable supply of school report pictures and articles for kids from kindergarten to college. (Trust me: You'll want to save these issues.)

NEW YORK BOTANICAL GARDEN

This 250-acre National Historic Landmark includes 16 specialty gardens, wetlands, ponds, a cascading waterfall, a 40-acre tract of the original forest that once covered New York City, dramatic rock outcroppings, and outstanding collections of orchids, daylilies, flowering trees, and conifers. But the reason families visit is the Everett Children's Adventure Garden, the first indoor/outdoor museum of botany and horticulture built especially for children. Its hands-on activities, imaginative exhibits, and fanciful gardens are exciting and inviting.

Stop at the visitor center for a free map and to check activity schedules. Then head for the Boulder Maze; explore its winding trail, and climb up to look through the discovery scope at the wetlands below. Next enter Beth's Maze, and find your way around the hedges. Sit or step on the oversize lily pads of the Sun, Dirt, and Water Gallery, and watch water shoot up. A giant frog topiary leaping from a splashing fountain welcomes you to discover how plants make food, move water, and use sunlight.

HEY, KIDS!

Don't miss the William and Lynda Steere Plant Discovery Center, in the Everett Children's Adventure Garden. Here you can become a real scientist doing experiments, examining plants through a microscope, and pressing plants. You can also have fun putting together giant plant jigsaw puzzles.

KEEP IN MIND The botanical garden is less crowded on weekdays, except Wednesday, when admission is free. A narrated tram tour, which runs every 30 minutes, lets you explore various places and spaces and reboard. Free guided walking tours on Wednesday, Thursday, Saturday, and Sunday as well as Monday holidays are probably best suited for older children. Weekend bird walks, at 12:30, are also free, as are audio tours of the conservatory's World of Plants, also available in a children's version.

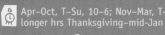
In the Children's Wonder Gallery, kids can play bamboo instruments, invent a plant, or wander through vine-covered tunnels, tiny bridges, and a minipond. At the outdoor Pond Gallery, kids can pretend to be a pond-dwelling animal. They can take a water sample and see what's in it, make a giant bird's nest, or visit the Plant Touch Tank.

The Children's Adventure Garden is part of the Children's Adventure Project, which also includes the Mitsubishi Wild Wetland Trail and the Ruth Rea Howell Family Garden. Along the wetland trail, children can get a close-up view of this fascinating ecosystem and discover What Stinks, an interactive exhibit about how wetlands recycle plants. In the family garden, visitors of all ages can dig; investigate ponds, insects, and plants; and meet gardeners from around the world.

The Enid A. Haupt Conservatory, the nation's largest Victorian glasshouse, showcases rain forest plants, desert galleries, and numerous palm trees under glass.

KID-FRIENDLY EATS The indoor/outdoor **Garden Cafe** serves kid-oriented comfort foods. Picnic tables are located at the Tulip Tree Terrace, near the Snuff Mill, on the Snuff Mill River Terrace, and outside the Children's Adventure Garden. Outside the garden in the Belmont section, also called Arthur Avenue, try one of the many pizza parlors and Italian restaurants. **Dominick's** (2335 Arthur Ave., tel. 718/733–2807) has inexpensive family-style Italian fare.

In a renovated three-story firehouse built in 1904, you and your family can view one of the most comprehensive collections of fire-related art and artifacts from the 18th century to the present. Large firehouse doors, the housewatch (front desk) entrance, stone floor, brass sliding pole, and hose tower remind visitors of the former home of Engine Company 30, its firefighters, its rigs, and its horses. The nonprofit museum operates in partnership with the New York City Fire Department, which owns the building and provides the collection and the firefighters who serve as tour guides.

Permanent and temporary exhibitions chronicle the evolution of fire-fighting technology beginning with the early bucket brigades. Carefully preserved hand-operated, horse-drawn, and motorized equipment; toys; models; fire engine lamps (running lights from horse-drawn equipment); presentation silver; oil paintings, prints, and photographs; "fire marks" (emblems on buildings denoting the brand of insurance carried); and folk art illuminate the traditions and lore of fire fighting.

HEY, KIDS! Create your own scavenger hunt. On the first floor, look for those wooden rattles used as the first fire alarms. Since dogs have always been firehouse mascots, search for a dog collar. Can you locate an early motorized fire truck that was started with a hand crank? On the second floor, find the fire chief's sleigh and the wagon with an eagle on top. This pumper rode in the parade for the newly unveiled Statue of Liberty over 100 years ago.

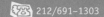

Organized fire fighting began in New York City in 1648, when eight fire wardens, nicknamed the Prowlers, patrolled the streets from dusk to dawn. These patrols were also called the Rattle Watch, as wooden rattles were the first fire alarms. Before phones were introduced in 1882, fire companies used the telegraph and a system of Morse code and bells to communicate fire emergencies across the city.

Preschoolers and early schoolers can learn why fires were a big problem in olden days and how bucket brigades worked. They may be fascinated by how men pulled and pumped the early fire wagons and how horses and dogs helped. They may also discover how fire fighting changed as New York grew from a small village to a large city. Older students may be interested in the evolution of fire alarms, in the duties of today's firefighters, and in the teamwork involved in fighting fires. To preview some of the museum's exhibits, visit its Web site at nyfd.com/museum.html.

KID-FRIENDLY EATS Hankering for some Cajun cooking and some cowgirl memorabilia? Head on over to the **Cowgirl Hall of Fame** (519 Hudson St., tel. 212/633–1133). On Monday night, it's all-you-can-eat at **Brothers Bar-B-Q** (225 Varick St., tel. 212/727–2775). Any day of the week, the kids will find this bilevel barnlike space just the place for chicken and ribs.

KEEP IN MIND Family workshops are available on a drop-in basis, whereas firefighter-led guided tours are by advance reservation. During a tour, you can visit a mock apartment equipped with lasers, black lights, theatrical smoke, and other devices simulating and highlighting common fire hazards. The building can get crowded when group tours visit, so call ahead to see if schools are scheduled when you're planning to come. The museum also hosts birthday parties for children 4–8. You can get fire-theme goodies from the museum store.

NEW YORK HALL OF SCIENCE

New York City's only hands-on science and technology museum is also one of the country's best. With more than 185 interactive exhibits over 35,000 indoor square feet (not to mention 30,000 outdoor square feet in the Science Playground), the hall is an exciting and inviting place to bring the family for a day of fun and learning.

The ground-level main exhibition hall contains the Seeing the Light exhibit and Sound Sensations: The Inside Story of Audio, where children jump, dance, and run while watching their shadows "play" music. They can also compose a jazz melody and electronically change their voices. (Next stop: pop radio!)

The lower level contains the Hidden Kingdoms of the World of Microbes, with the largest collection of the world's smallest creatures. Also here are the Realm of the Atom and Marvelous Molecules—The Secret of Life, devoted to the shared chemistry of all living things.

HEY, KIDS!

Don't miss the Science Playground (April–November), the Western Hemisphere's largest outdoor laboratory of exciting whole-body experiences. Compose a tune with your feet on Sound Steps. Talk softly into the red Whisper Dish, and marvel when a friend across the playground can hear you.

KEEP IN MIND

Built for the 1964–65 New York World's Fair, this facility does not permit strollers. Baby carriers are available, as are wheelchairs (the museum is wheelchair accessible). Students with A's in both math and science can receive a free one-year Honors Membership, and budding scientists might also want to test the hypothesis that a gift shop purchase will help them remember a day in the realm of the sciences.

The upper level's Great Hall is home to traveling exhibitions. In the kid-pleasing bubble area, you and yours can create life-size bubbles or raise a bubble wall. Proceed with caution or you'll burst your bubble! From the Great Hall, exit outside to the Science Playground.

A state-of-the-art 300-seat auditorium serves as a showcase for videos, films, lectures, and special events. Live science demonstrations are scheduled daily throughout the facility, and helpful staffers are stationed on all floors to demonstrate exhibits and otherwise assist you.

In the Preschool Discovery Place, little hands can investigate sound, color and light, simple machines, and measurement in a special self-contained space apart from the bustling crowds that can be alarming to the under-6 crowd. For the over-6 crowd, a multimedia science library houses an extensive collection of books, videos, periodicals, CD-ROMS, and table-top activities.

KID-FRIENDLY EATS Pack a lunch and find a spot in the spacious 300-seat **dining hall** overlooking the park and Science Playground. No time to make a bag lunch? You can also purchase sandwiches, snacks, and beverages once you get there. The dining hall is available for children's birthday parties. **The Park Side** (107-01 Corona Ave., tel. 718/271–9276) offers big portions of excellent Italian food served by a helpful staff.

NEW YORK LIBERTY BASKET-BALL

I t's fast-paced, it's fun, it's family entertainment, and it's affordable. If this doesn't sound like today's professional sports to you, you haven't been to a New York Liberty game. The area's hot WNBA (Women's National Basketball Association) team plays summer basketball to Madison Square Garden crowds of just under 20,000, averaging second in overall attendance in the WNBA. It's not uncommon to spot celebrities like model Tyra Banks, actors Gregory Hines or Billy Baldwin, or talk-show host Rosie O'Donnell in the crowd.

Each season has 32 games, with half played at home at the Garden. Games usually run under two hours, unless overtime is called. Arrive early—gates open one hour before game time—to watch the pregame shoot-around and team warm-up. Technically, no photographs are permitted, but young fans with cameras do snap shots of their favorite players before the games. Save the complimentary souvenir roster cards, given out at every game. These cards will help your kids keep track of their favorite player and her game statistics. Souvenir team yearbooks are $3.

HEY, KIDS! Hey basketball fans and Web surfers, log on to www.nyliberty.com to check out a cool way to catch up with your favorite team. You can e-mail questions to the team's head athletic trainer or e-mail your questions directly to the team. There's a Kids Book Club section and other features that will take you behind the scenes to learn all about the team and the game they play.

 Madison Square Garden, 7th Ave. between
31st and 33rd Sts.

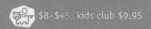 $8–$45, kids club $9.95

 212/564–WNBA Liberty Hotline,
201/784–9600 kids club

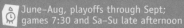 June–Aug, playoffs through Sept;
games 7:30 and Sa–Su late afternoon

 5 and up

Another way to keep up with Liberty is to join the Liberty Kids Club. Members receive the "Rookie Report," the club's official newsletter; a membership certificate; membership card; folders; stickers; birthday greetings; and more.

During the games, look for Maddie the Mascot, a friendly overgrown dog, making friends with the fans, leading the conga lines on the court, and leading the cheers. Also part of the excitement here is the 12-member Torch Patrol. This athletic, high-energy squad of young men and women conduct fun, frenzied mayhem during time-outs, incorporating tumbling, dance, and crowd interaction. And don't even think about leaving your seat during halftime, or you'll miss the entertainment. When was the last time you got to see Frisbee-catching dogs or bike stunts? Don't try this at home! But do practice your hook shot and keep dribbling.

KID-FRIENDLY EATS The **Houlihan's** (2 Pennsylvania Plaza, tel. 212/630–0349) chain of restaurants is known for its kid-friendly fare, balloons, crayons, and appealing adult menu. There's one at Penn Station. Another chain known for its family cuisine is **T.G.I. Friday's** (484 8th Ave., tel. 212/630–0307). Go for the burgers, sandwiches, or salads.

KEEP IN MIND Promotions take place during certain games. Whether it's miniball or sports-poster giveaways, mascot day or fan appreciation T-shirt night, these special events give your kids another highlight just by walking through the turnstile. The team also holds celebrations like Flag Day, Father's Day, and charitable game promotions like a Cheering for Children Auction and Breast Cancer Awareness Night. Check the Web site for updates, and if you have a choice, pick a game where they're giving something away.

NEW YORK TRANSIT MUSEUM

When is a museum not an ordinary museum? When it's housed in a decommissioned 1936 subway station in downtown Brooklyn. The New York Transit Museum is a walk-up, sit-down, and touch museum that is the home to 100 years of transit history and memorabilia. The collections include 19 restored subway cars dating from 1904 to 1964, as well as antique turnstiles, a working signal tower, a surface transportation room, and a variety of other transit equipment.

Revolving exhibits, programs, workshops, and tours provide an insider's look at MTA bridges, tunnels, subways, buses, and commuter railroads. You and your children can watch a film clip about the age of Els (elevated trains) before they fade into history. Take the A Train or catch all the trains you missed in an exhibit of full-size classic wooden cars and their modern counterparts. Or see a sign of the times in a display of nearly 200 examples of subway signage: in porcelain enamel, cast iron, brass, wood, and plastic. Pass through the first automated turnstiles. Drive a city bus, or better yet, don't miss the museum's annual Bus Festival,

KID-FRIENDLY EATS The **Armando Ristorante** (143 Montague St., tel. 718/624–7167) offers traditional Italian fare at more than fair prices. For other food choices, *see* the Brooklyn Academy of Music and Brooklyn Botanic Garden.

KEEP IN MIND The museum offers guided tours of different parts of the transit system in Manhattan, the Bronx, Queens, Brooklyn, Staten Island, and Long Island, and some include excursions to historical and cultural destinations. Because some tours involve strenuous walking and stair climbing, wear sturdy and comfortable shoes and clothes. Bring your MetroCard or tokens for travel, but first call ahead for reservation information and fees.

Boerum Pl. and Schermerhorn St.,
Brooklyn Heights

 718/243–8601

 $3 adults, $1.50 children
3–17; some workshops
have materials fees

T–F 10–4, Sa–Su 12–5

2 and up

in late spring or early summer. An entire block is shut to park historic buses outside, including a wooden open-top double-decker bus and a favorite, the 1949 Jackie Gleason bus, modeled after the one driven by Ralph Kramden on the *Honeymooners*.

Shopping for a (subway) token of your affection to give to a (nostalgic) loved one? Look no further than the Transit Museum Store. (Along with the shop located inside the museum, there are stores in Grand Central Station adjacent to the Station Masters' Office and at the Times Square Visitors Center, on the east side of Broadway between 46th and 47th streets.) If you're looking for transit-related toys, trinkets, and memorabilia, this is the place.

HEY, KIDS! Each year the museum conducts some nifty workshops just for kids. You can build a working model of a suspension bridge, make your own bus model, or create poetry in motion by writing your own poster poem like the ones on subways and buses. Or sign up for a special workshop with New York City Transit engineer Vinny Voltage (Vollano). His science sessions include chemistry, physics, electricity, and mechanics in an awesome and magical demonstration not to be missed.

NEW YORK UNEARTHED

It's not every day that you can get down in the dirt in the middle of New York City without a reprimand from Mom or Dad. New York Unearthed is a museum experience filled with New York's archaeological heritage, where the remains of the past tell the story of New York's colorful history. The program operates under the auspices of the South Street Seaport Museum and focuses on interpreting the life of New Yorkers through the objects they left behind.

Don't miss the Unearthing New York Systems Elevator, which whisks your family down through the layers of a simulated dig beneath the city streets. Your children can explore a three-dimensional cross-section of an archaeological site and view archaeologists and conservators at work in a glass-enclosed state-of-the-art laboratory. The urban history program allows aspiring archaeologists to dig in a simulated site via a portable "dig box" seeded with artifacts. They can excavate the artifacts, screen, record, and interpret their findings under the supervision of the archaeology staff.

HEY, KIDS! Time travel is possible when you spend a week at the South Street Seaport Museum's Dig It! Archaeology Camp. You can discover the amazing secrets buried beneath the skyscrapers of New York in five-day sessions, offered during July and August for kids 8–11. Campers piece together artifacts, make crafts, meet special guests, play 19th-century games, and take a lunch cruise along the East River on archaeological adventures. Space is limited to 15 per session.

 17 State St., at Battery Park, in courtyard on Pearl between Whitehall and State Sts.

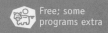 Free; some programs extra

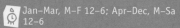 Jan–Mar, M–F 12–6; Apr–Dec, M–Sa 12–6

 212/748–8628; 212/748–8590 for programs

 4 and up

The archaeological collections of eight nearby scientifically excavated urban sites include approximately 7,000 exhibit-quality artifacts as well as over 2 million associated artifacts. These items help illuminate the worlds of merchants, artisans, slave traders, slaves, seamen and their families, grocers, boardinghouse keepers, and the children who lived in lower Manhattan from the days of New Amsterdam to the early 20th century.

Public programs include demonstrations, lectures, performances, workshops, walking tours, and guided museum tours, which focus on the themes of tenement life, early tools, 17th- to 19th-century diet, artisans' workshops, and trade. In a city bursting with unusual experiences, this one is truly unique, and as hard as it is to believe, admission is free. Can you dig it?

KID-FRIENDLY EATS Offering coffee and other coffee-based drinks, sandwiches, and snacks, **New World Coffee** (100 Wall St., tel. 212/514–5011) is a good place for an inexpensive bite. Visit **Souperman** (77 Pearl St., tel. 212/269–5777) for "souperb" lunchtime takeout.

KEEP IN MIND New York Unearthed has expanded programming to provide educational experiences for all ages—from preschoolers to seniors. Founded on the belief that people learn in many ways, the exhibits and activities here are not only age appropriate but also appeal to different learning styles through visual, tactile, and auditory stimulation. Grandparents and great-grandparents can perhaps relate what they see to what they lived or heard about, so why not bring them along to enrich everyone's experience?

NY WATERWAY FERRIES

In the early 1800s, New Yorkers traveled to and from Manhattan by ferry, but as bridges and tunnels were constructed, ferries fell out of favor. Today, you can experience this form of transportation on NY Waterway, the largest private ferry operation in the nation. NY Waterway transports over 6 million passengers into the city each year on 20 boats with over a dozen ferry routes. For commuters, ferries offer a shortcut to Manhattan minus the traffic jams, tunnel and bridge tolls, and parking problems usually associated with car travel. Ferry crossings run anywhere from five to eight minutes, with frequent departures throughout the day.

Ferries aren't just for commuters, however. If your family wants to sightsee, you can take a fun-filled ride and glide to ports of call in and around New York—to the beach at Sandy Hook, New Jersey; around lower Manhattan; up the Hudson River; and off to LaGuardia Airport, just to name a few. Most terminals offer all-day parking, and a free private shuttle bus system operates throughout the city, providing service to tourists, commuters, and downtown residents.

HEY, KIDS!

If you're taking a ferry to a Yankee game, why not make it a double-header of sorts? Ask your parents to find out about tours of Yankee Stadium (tel. 718/579–4531). Highlights include the dugout, press box, clubhouse, and Monument Park.

KEEP IN MIND

The best sightseeing bargain in the city is the free 20- to 30-minute ride on the Staten Island Ferry (tel. 718/390–5253) across New York Harbor. Take the older model blue and orange ferries, which sail higher in the water and have outside deck space, so you can enjoy views of the Manhattan skyline, the Statue of Liberty, Ellis Island, the New Jersey shore, and the Verrazano Narrows Bridge. Ferries run every 15 minutes during rush hours, every 20–30 minutes most other times of the day and evening, and every hour after 11 PM and on weekend mornings.

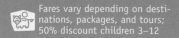

Sightseeing tours around lower Manhattan include harbor cruises by day and twilight cruises providing up-close views of the Statue of Liberty, Ellis Island, and the Brooklyn Bridge. You can also take a ferry to see the Mets or Yankees play ball. Packages include ferry transportation, a ticket to the game, a hot dog and beverage, and a souvenir. Dining and Broadway show packages are also available.

Hudson River cruises include tours of the legendary Rockefeller family estate in Pocantico Hills and historic Philipsburg Manor, a working Dutch Colonial farm; a Sleepy Hollow Cruise, including Sunnyside, the home of Washington Irving, and Philipsburg Manor; a scenic trip down the North Hudson River without stops; and a cruise to Lynhurst, a great Gothic revival–style estate. But as nice as these sights are, what's really special about the tours is seeing New York from the water.

KID-FRIENDLY EATS Some boats have a snack bar selling snacks, soft drinks, and cocktails. On some sightseeing cruises, box lunches are served, and passengers often take them ashore and eat at the historic sight being visited. Dining packages include reservations at various city restaurants. If you're taking NY Waterway from Weehawken, New Jersey's Port Imperial Terminal, consider eating at **Arthur's Landing** (Pershing Rd., Weehawken, NJ, tel. 201/867–0777), which has a kids' menu.

OPERA AT LINCOLN CENTER

No need to sing the praises of opera when you can experience it with your family at Lincoln Center. New York's amazing performing arts center is filled with theaters of all shapes and sizes, playing host to every type of music imaginable, dance, film, and even the circus. Of these, opera is perhaps the least accessible for many children, but not to worry. Two programs at the center, both geared to families, offer introductions to this musical and theatrical art form.

Through its education department, New York City Opera offers one-hour interactive workshops prior to select weekend matinee performances. City Opera staff and artists conduct hands-on activities that explore the themes, drama, and music of the afternoon's opera, and everyone is encouraged to join in the fun, which may include acting out a scene, learning a dance, crafting a costume, or exploring a musical score. Four family-friendly operas are usually chosen each season. Past sessions have included such operas as *Hansel and Gretel, Cunning Little Vixen,* and Puccini's *La Boheme.* Advance reservations are required for the workshops, held at the New York State Theater; doors, at the stage entrance, open at 11:30.

KEEP IN MIND Like its bubbling, dancing fountain, Lincoln Center is overflowing with wonderful family performances, from jazz to the circus, ballet to movies. Here's just a handful: the Chamber Music Society's Meet the Music Concerts for Kids (tel. 212/875–5788), Jazz at Lincoln Center (tel. 212/875–5599), the Little Orchestra Society's Happy Concerts for Young People (tel. 212/769–7000), Movies for Kids (tel. 212/875–5610), and the New York City Philharmonic's Young People's Concerts (tel. 212/721–6500).

 Weekend workshops, New York State Theater, 62nd St. and Columbus Ave.

 Weekend workshops Sa–Su 12–1

212/870–5643 weekend workshops, 212/769–7008 Growing Up with Opera

 Weekend workshops $8; Growing Up with Opera under $20

Weekend workshops 6–12, Growing Up with Opera 4–12

The Metropolitan Opera Guild annually presents its series, Growing Up with Opera, a perfect premiere operatic experience for budding enthusiasts. The series is staged at smaller kid-friendly theaters and comprises three productions sung in English: one especially designed for 4 to 6 year-olds and two for 6 to 12 year-olds. Each year one of these performances is an updated classic opera, edited to a family-friendly length. A home activity book ($5)—filled with puzzles, games, engaging explanations, and fun facts—is available for this opera by calling in advance or purchasing it prior to the performance. Immediately following the performance of the classic opera, you can opt to join the cast for a party ($5 admits four) with cookies, punch, and balloons. Children receive a cast photo and can scurry about, meeting (and collecting autographs from) their favorite costumed performers. It's a memorable finale to the opera.

KID-FRIENDLY EATS To end your trip on a good note, try **Opera Espresso Restaurant** (1928 Broadway, tel. 212/799–3050). This glorified diner is accommodating to families, offering everything from chicken fingers to French cuisine. To see why New Yorkers sing the praises of its brick-oven pizza, visit **John's Pizzeria** (48 W. 65th St., tel. 212/721–7001).

HEY, KIDS! If your interest has been piqued by the magic of opera, ask a parent if you can take a backstage tour of the Metropolitan Opera House (tel. 212/769–7020). Marvel at castle construction in the carpentry shop, see suits of armor and Cinderella gowns sewn in the costume shop, and peruse big hair and bald pates at the wig-maker's shop. Peek into the rehearsal room, auditorium, dressing rooms, and the cafeteria. Tours, for those 8 and up, are weekday afternoons and Saturday mornings.

PLAYSPACE

If it's raining, it's pouring, and it's getting boring, pack up your rambunctious youngsters, and head to PlaySpace, the city's first walk-in indoor playground just for kids 6 and under. Here they can jump, run, dig, play, sing, slide, eat, crawl, skip, splash, tumble, hop, laugh, and talk to their hearts' content (and yours).

PlaySpace contains all sorts of areas that appeal to youngsters with all sorts of interests. There's plenty of room for an Olympic-size sandbox; a two-story firehouse; train and water tables; a toddler labyrinth; a 6-foot twisting slide; bridges, tunnels, and other climbing structures; a child-size stage; dress-up costumes; and more! There are also weekly events and crafts activities.

PlaySpace is not just a place for parents to sit and kids to run around. There's plenty of opportunity for parent and child interaction, creativity, and fun—all in a clean, safe, and challenging free-play environment. Huge age-specific play areas, storytelling, arts and crafts, child-size hoops, and tons of toys round out the experience.

HEY, KIDS!

In addition to plain-old play, PlaySpace offers varied classes. Topics include music, ballet, drama, art, computers, and baby games. (You can even tell Mom and Dad that they offer parenting workshops.) So find out what's coming up. You might want to learn before (or after) you leap.

KEEP IN MIND For other indoor playgrounds, like **Rain or Shine** (115 E. 29th St., tel. 212/432–4420), check the Yellow Pages. For older children, try sports and recreation centers: **Hackers, Hitters & Hoops** (123 W. 18th St., tel. 212/929–7482) features batting cages, Ping-Pong, basketball, an obstacle course, video games, and miniature golf. **LaZerPark** (1560 Broadway, tel. 212/398–3060) has LaZer Tag and video, arcade, and token games. **ExtraVertical Climbing Center** (61 W. 62nd St., tel. 212/586–5382) is an indoor climbing gym for beginners to experienced climbers.

2473 Broadway, at 92nd St.

 212/769-2300

 $6.50 players

M–Sa 9:30–6, Su 10–6

6 mth–6 yr

The staff is warm and welcoming, and the rest rooms—containing changing stations and a kid-size bathroom—are clean. Safety flooring protects against injury from falls and tumbles, and for summer comfort, the complex is air-conditioned. You'll probably also be happy to know that all equipment and toys are disinfected nightly and the sandbox is raked daily, sifted once a week, and changed every month. Now if only they'd had a place like this when you were a kid!

KID-FRIENDLY EATS PlaySpace has a healthy **snack bar** on the premises for parents and kids. **Boulevard** (2398 Broadway, tel. 212/874–7400) is a brassiere-style eatery where kids can slurp spaghetti and draw on the tablecloths. The **Popover Cafe** (551 Amsterdam Ave., tel. 212/595–8555) is very child friendly, dotted with teddy bears in various nooks and crannies. Comfortable booths and hearty food welcome family diners.

PROSPECT PARK

Prospect Park offers over 500 acres of winding paths, rolling hills, open spaces, and great green places to stroll, picnic, fly a kite, feed the ducks, or sit and think. Modeled after Central Park, it is home to the 75-acre Long Meadow, one of the city's greatest open spaces, with spectacular views of grass, trees, and sky. Feed the ducks and spot the swans at 60-acre Prospect Lake, or stroll through the Flower Garden and Oriental Pavilion.

If you want to ice-skate, head for the Kate Wollman Center and Rink from mid-November to early March, near the Lincoln Road entrance. Skate rental is available as is instruction, offered by the New York Skating Center. Most of the rest of the year, this is the place to rent pedal boats, which seat four—a great way to take a break and a tour of the lake at the same time.

A 1912 carousel, in operation from April to October but not every day, features 51 magnificently carved wooden horses, along with a lion, giraffe, deer, and dragon-drawn chariots. It is located

HEY, KIDS! For a haunting good time, join the Halloween Haunted Walk and Festival held at Prospect Park the last Saturday in October from noon until 3; it's near the Nethermead (the geographical center of the park). You'll be in ghoulish company as thousands of visitors walk along the haunted park pathways. Watch out for witches, ghosts, goblins, and other creatures that go bump in the night—or, in this case, the afternoon. Don't miss the kiddie carnival with games and prizes.

 Eastern Pkwy. and Grand Army
Plaza, Brooklyn

 718/855–7882 park, 718/965–
6505 children's museum

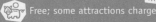 Free; some attractions charge

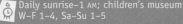 Daily sunrise–1 AM; children's museum
W–F 1–4, Sa–Su 1–5

 9 mth and up

at the Willink entrance at the intersection of Empire Boulevard and Flatbush Avenue. For live animals, head to the Prospect Park Wildlife Center (*see below*).

Last but certainly not least is the Lefferts Homestead Children's Museum, in one of the few surviving Dutch Colonial farmhouses in Brooklyn. Today it plays home to kids who play house in this historic building. Though there are two period rooms furnished with antiques, your children can play in four rooms furnished with reproduction furniture, interactive toys, and games. A dollhouse replica of the Lefferts Homestead provides another way to play with the past. Seasonal programs, storytelling, theater, and music are ongoing throughout the year, and family volunteer programs offer opportunities for families to work, play, and learn together.

KEEP IN MIND
Prospect Park hosts special community events throughout the year, including a Girl Scout Jamboree, ethnic parades, and festivals. The free Celebrate Brooklyn Concerts are held at the Bandshell (Prospect Park West and 9th St.) from mid-June through Labor Day. Music for young and old ranges from jazz to bluegrass, classical to zydeco.

KID-FRIENDLY EATS A short walk from the Bandshell, the **Living Room Cafe** (199 Prospect Park West, tel. 718/389–0824) is located in the historic Pavilion Theater, once a single-screen movie house but now a multiplex. Have a sandwich, a sundae, an egg cream, or crepes as you watch the strollers in the park. **Kate's Corner Snack Bar** (Kate Wollman Center and Rink) is open Thursday through Sunday.

PROSPECT PARK WILDLIFE CENTER

This 12-acre zoo, completely revamped and transformed into a state-of-the-art children's wildlife learning lab, is home to 82 species of animals. Naturalistic habitat exhibits have replaced bars, cages, and pits, and the larger species that were part of the original menagerie of the late 1800s and early 1900s are gone.

Enter the Animals Lifestyles building, and your children will find air, water, and land animals in exhibits related to the center's wildlife education program. Reptiles, amphibians, fish, birds, and small mammals help highlight the environments they live in and their adaptations to their homes. The centerpiece of the building is the 4,500-square-foot hamadryas baboon exhibit. Perched high on the rock cliffs by an impressive waterfall, separated from these fascinating social primates by an invisible sheet of glass, their somewhat less fascinating primate cousins (humans) feel very much a part of this exhibit. Don't be surprised if a friendly baboon approaches the glass to study you back!

TRANSPORTATION There are entrances—one off Flatbush Avenue and one near the Lefferts Homestead. If you drive, you can find free parking on Flatbush Avenue. By public transportation, take the subway's D train to the Prospect Park station or the B41, B47, or B48 bus.

KID-FRIENDLY EATS A **cafeteria** is near the sea lion pool. Visit the **Second Street Cafe** (189 7th Ave., tel. 718/369–6928) for lunch or brunch. Order soup and some raisin-studded bread pudding. Try **Two Boots** (514 2nd St., tel. 718/499–3253) for creative pizzas (including Cajun), pasta jambalaya (for adventurous kids), paper tablecloths, coloring books, crayons, and a rest room changing table. (Can you guess why it's called Two Boots?) Other neighborhood kid fare is listed under the Brooklyn Botanic Garden.

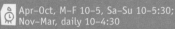
Drawing supplies are provided and sketches invited in the Animals in Our Lives building. Playful meerkats, scarlet macaws, saw-whet owls, and red-eyed tree frogs call this space their home. In a second area, friendly staffers discuss pet care and what species should *not* be domesticated. In an outdoor barnyard, your kids can peek into the chicken coop or meet the goats, sheep, and cows up close and personal. The California sea lions now frolic in a rocky California coast–like environment with a refurbished pool double the size of their former home.

Innovative prekindergarten programs have inviting themes like Bedtime at the Barn, Baboon Breakfast, and Animal Crackers. Other kids' programs are available on a first-come, first-served basis through mail-in registration. Some run over school vacations or overnight and have included a Spooky Sleepover, Zoo Dreams, and a Polar Pack-In. The wildlife center also sponsors special community events—the Fleece Festival, Animal Mystery Weekend, Boo at the Zoo, and the Winter Solstice Celebration—free with admission. All in all, it makes for wonderful family fun.

HEY, KIDS! Want to really experience animal habitats? Visit the World of Animals's 2½-acre Discovery Trail. Burrow in Plexiglas-topped tunnels, and pop up next to a prairie dog. Leap-frog across lily pads to goose nests, and pretend to hatch. In the Wallaby Walkabout, you can walk among these small Australian kangaroos and other animals, and in the 2,500-foot aviary at trail's end, you can walk around free-flying African birds and climb into nests your size. Willoughby Wallaby Whew!

PUPPETWORKS

For more than 35 years, the Puppetworks, Inc., under the artistic direction of Nicolas Coppola, has been known throughout the country for its mostly marionette productions. In 1987 Puppetworks opened a permanent 75-seat theater in a Park Slope (Brooklyn) storefront, conveniently located next to the Puppetworks workshop. Puppet performances are also staged at the Children's Aid Society's Greenwich Village Center Theater. These informal and family-friendly theaters present daily performances of children's literature classics, with weekdays reserved for groups (20 or more).

Favorites like *Puss in Boots, Rumpelstiltskin,* and *Pinocchio* may round out a year-round season that might also include the *Wizard of Oz,* a gala *Carnival of the Animals, The Frog Prince, Peter and the Wolf,* and the *Emperor's Nightingale.*

Just two puppeteers are responsible for each show, and while each show averages 13 puppet characters, some shows have had up to 68 puppets in one performance! The professionally

KEEP IN MIND Since1976, when Macy's built a gingerbread puppet theater for Puppetworks, more than 50,000 children and their families have attended the annual Puppetworks Christmas performances. Bring your family to the ninth floor of Macy's Herald Square (Broadway at 34th St., tel. 212/695–4400), and start a new tradition. The holiday-theme performances are given Tuesday through Sunday 10 times each day and cost only a few dollars. In 1999 Macy's built a new puppet theater for these always festive and well-attended family puppet programs.

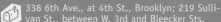 338 6th Ave., at 4th St., Brooklyn; 219 Sullivan St., between W. 3rd and Bleecker Sts.

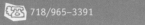 718/965-3391

Brooklyn $7 adults, $5 children under 18; Manhattan $8 adults, $5 children

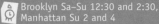 Brooklyn Sa–Su 12:30 and 2:30, Manhattan Su 2 and 4

 2–12

designed sets and intricate puppet costumes give the feeling of a "slightly scaled-down" Broadway show. At the end of many performances, one of the professional puppeteers will bring out a puppet to show to the audience, giving a brief behind-the-scenes—or, more accurately, above-the-strings—talk about the workings of a puppet theater.

In the spirit of artistic cooperation, other puppeteering troupes from across the country often appear here, too.

KID-FRIENDLY EATS In the Village, try coal-fired pizza at **Arturo's** (106 W. Houston St., tel. 212/677-3820) or tempting soups and sandwiches at **Aggie's** (146 W. Houston St., tel. 212/673-8994). In Park Slope, **Two Boots** (*see* Prospect Park Wildlife Center) has Italian and Cajun cooking at its best. For crispy, thin pizza go to **Lento's** (833 Union St., tel. 718/399-8782).

HEY, KIDS! The walls of the Brooklyn Puppetworks theater display close to 100 marionettes used in past performances, though many are re-used and re-costumed. Can you identify the characters or the stories they come from? If you can't, let your imagination wander. Try to think of fairy tales you know. Who's the scariest villain, the cutest animal, your favorite character? Do any of the puppets you see look like them, and how do they differ from the way you would have created them?

QUEENS COUNTY FARM MUSEUM

15

A farm in New York City? Just barely. At the very edge of Queens, the Queens County Farm Museum occupies New York City's largest remaining tract of natural, undisturbed farmland. The landmark farmhouse and the 7-acre farmyard that make up the museum are just a small piece of the 47-acre Adriance Farm Park.

The farm was started in 1772 and passed through a series of owners until 1927, when New York State purchased the farm for Creedmoor Psychiatric Hospital, to provide both fresh produce and therapy for its patients. Staff and patients raised crops and livestock until the program was discontinued in 1960. Through the Colonial Farmhouse Restoration Society of Bellerose, organized in 1975, the farm's historic structures were preserved and the site was turned into a city park.

Pick up a map and take a self-guiding tour of the farm museum. Begin at the centerpiece of the restored farm: the colonial farmhouse, where much of the original 18th-century

HEY, KIDS!

Contribute to the Fund-A-Friend program, and you'll get a certificate and your name will be included on a display at the farm. Funds raised are used for feed and veterinary care, from $8 for a chicken or duck to $100 annually for a "caretaker," helping all the animals.

KEEP IN MIND Of the many family programs here, most carry a fee and some require reservations. Activities have included a fall Apple Festival, Barnyard Easter Egg Hunt, arts and crafts workshops in winter and spring, New York's Annual Antique Auto Show, a weekend Civil War encampment, the Queens County Fair, and the Thunderbird American Indian Mid-Summer Pow Wow. A summer program of arts, crafts, and nature courses for children 6–10, comprising three two-week sessions, is offered, as are one-hour summer arts and crafts workshops for children 4–5.

plank floors, beamed ceilings, wainscoting, paneling, doors, window glass, and hardware has survived. Other areas available for touring include the duck pond, the herb garden, and the orchard. A chicken coop houses 100 free-range hens producing 260–290 large brown eggs each laying cycle. The eggs are collected daily and washed and boxed for sale. Your children can visit Daisy, an Ayreshire cow, in the cow shed and stroll by the sheep pastures to survey the grazing livestock. Fields are planted with corn, pumpkins, tomatoes, and other vegetables.

Each season the farm wears a new face, whether it's welcoming newborn barn animals in spring or picking the fresh produce of summer, stomping through the snow paths in winter or crunching a crispy autumn apple. The Queens County Farm Museum offers a thick slice of farm life to you and your family, painting a picture of the city's rich agricultural past.

KID-FRIENDLY EATS You can't beat the price or the selection at the lunch buffet at **Pizza Hut** (253-11 Hillside Ave., Bellerose, tel. 718/343–1118). Add in kids' meals, and you can feed a child for under $3 and yourself for under $6. Hop on over to **IHOP** (248-16 Northern Blvd., Little Neck, tel. 718/224–1178), short for the International House of Pancakes, to indulge in breakfast all day long. It's a surefire bet for pancake lovers, especially kids who love different flavored syrups.

QUEENS WILDLIFE CENTER

Once upon a time, Flushing Meadow played host to the 1964 World's Fair. A zoo opened on the fairgrounds in 1968, and in 1992 it was completely revamped, transforming itself into this small but friendly wildlife center. The 11-acre zoo is home to 400 animals of some 40 species. Here you can come face to face with a mountain lion, see American black bears at play, and watch Roosevelt elk roaming the range.

In fact, you can walk on the wild side from one coast of the United States to the other. Visit re-created habitats from a northeastern forest to the Great Plains to the rocky California coast. Stroll from the forest floor to the treetops of the center's walk-through aviary (a geodesic dome designed by Buckminster Fuller for the World's Fair) to view a variety of birds. Cross the covered viewing bridge of the coyote exhibit to peek into a window on their world.

The marsh exhibit forms a habitat for ducks, geese, herons, egrets, and turtles. The bison range lets you watch these fascinating American symbols from various points, giving the

HEY, KIDS! When school's out, the wildlife center is in. Arts and crafts and other special events take place weekends and holidays from 1 to 4. Most activities are free with admission. Past favorites have included Sheep-Shearing Weekend, Bison Bonanza, Turkey Time, and Eagle Weekend. Kids to Kritters programs, for youngsters 3–5, include exploration of animal homes, arts and crafts, storytelling, animal demonstrations, and zoo tours. These one-hour sessions do charge a fee for children and adults.

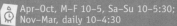

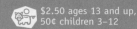

53-51 111th St., Flushing Meadow Corona Park, Flushing, Queens

718/271-7761

$2.50 ages 13 and up, 50¢ children 3-12

Apr–Oct, M–F 10–5, Sa–Su 10–5:30; Nov–Mar, daily 10–4:30

All ages

effect of the Great Plains of long ago. A new waterfall, additional trees, and rock formations have improved the habitat for the endangered South American spectacled bears. Don't forget to say hi to Claire, the bald eagle named for Queens Borough President Claire Shulman.

On the domestic side of the center, youngsters can meet and touch goats, sheep, and rabbits in an inviting planted space where they can also see a llama, Vietnamese pot-bellied pig, zebu, Jersey steer, fawn, and such feathered friends as a Peking duck and Rhode Island red. Despite its size, the zoo offers something for just about everyone.

KID-FRIENDLY EATS Work up an animal appetite and visit the **cafeteria,** which overlooks the sea lion pool. Or visit **Uncle George's** (33-19 Broadway, Astoria, tel. 718/626–0593) for cheap, hearty, home-style diner cuisine at its best. Or try the **Omonia Cafe** (32-20 Broadway, Astoria, tel. 718/274–6650) for a light bite and people-watching on Broadway.

KEEP IN MIND The Queens Wildlife Center is located next to the New York Hall of Science, both in Flushing Meadow Corona Park. Combine your visit to either place with a stop at the nearby Queens Museum of Art (New York City Building, tel. 718/592–9700) to see the 9,335-square-foot scale model of New York City—complete with 895,000 tiny buildings and landmarks—originally made for the 1964 World's Fair.

RADIO CITY MUSIC HALL

You may have watched an awards show broadcast from Radio City Music Hall or even attended a performance here yourself, but to really get behind the scenes of this lavish Art Deco palace that's home to the high-kicking, smart-stepping Rockettes, you'll want to take the Grand Tour. The brainchild of theatrical impresario S. L. "Roxy" Rothafel, owner of New York's Roxy Theater, Radio City was the first building in the Rockefeller Center complex and the world's largest indoor theater in 1932. Tour guides take you on a journey that showcases the building's technological capabilities as well as the history of many performances that occurred here over the decades.

To whet your appetite, here are some amazing Radio City facts: Did you know that some of the curtains at Radio City can create steam and rain on stage and that the shimmering gold curtain is the largest theatrical curtain on earth? The mighty Wurlitzer organ, built in 1932, has two consoles, each weighing 2½ tons. It takes 11 rooms to house the pipes for this musical marvel, and some pipes are as much as 32 feet tall! Look up and you'll see a 24-

HEY, KIDS!

Imagine all the people and events that have graced this famous stage: from Madonna to Barney, the MTV Video Music Awards to the Tonys. *Snow White and the Seven Dwarfs* (1938) and *101 Dalmatians* (1996) were premiered here on the world's largest conventional screen.

KEEP IN MIND

In 1979, to save the music hall from the wrecking ball, the program format was changed from films and stage shows to live concerts, television specials, and events. The *Radio City Christmas Spectacular*, *Sesame Street Live*, and adult as well as kid concerts play to sell-out crowds throughout the year. We're guessing you probably won't get an invitation to a big awards show, so you'll have to pay to attend one of these performances if you want to see a show at this extraordinary venue. It's worth the price.

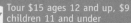
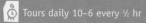

carat gold-leaf ceiling glistening 60 feet above your head. For the electrical record, the music hall contains over 25,000 light bulbs inside; outside, the marquee is a block long and has more than 6 miles of red and blue neon.

The tour also includes a visit to the private apartment of founder Roxy Rothafel and a stop in the costume shop, which contains examples of some of the lustrous outfits worn by the Rockettes over the years. Your tour group will also meet a member of the world's most renowned precision dance troupe, who will share some of the company's history. One-hour tours depart every ½ hour from the main lobby at the corner of 6th Avenue and 50th Street.

And once your family has taken the tour, consider coming back for a performance to see all that technological wizardry at work.

KID-FRIENDLY EATS Take your pick (or your children's pick) of local theme restaurants, each with eye-appealing memorabilia and kid fare. Music fans sing the praises of the **Hard Rock Cafe** (221 W. 57th St., tel. 212/459–9320). Movie buffs marvel at **Planet Hollywood** (140 W. 57th St., tel. 212/333–7827). And don't forget to doo-wop at the **Motown Cafe** (104 W. 57th St., tel. 212/581–8030).

ROCKEFELLER CENTER AND THE ICE RINK

I t's enchanting, its twinkling, it's festive and fun, and when the huge Christmas tree presides over the Ice Rink at Rockefeller Plaza, it's spectacular. It may not be the biggest rink in the world, but skating here certainly is one of the big New York experiences. Skate and locker rentals, season passes and multiticket books, lessons, and group rates are all available. Teens get a bit exuberant during evening skates and the pace is faster, but day or night, it's a skate to remember.

But the ice rink is just a small part of the 22-acre complex known as Rockefeller Center, one of the world's most famous pieces of real estate. There are actually 19 limestone and aluminum buildings here. Before or after your skating session, travel this complex moving east to west, following a trail punctuated by three famous statues from Greek mythology. Atlas stands guard outside the International Building (5th Ave. between 50th and 51st Sts.). Head one block south on 5th Avenue and turn west to stroll along the Channel Gardens, which lead from 5th Avenue to a stair connected to the Lower Plaza. Six rock pools are

KEEP IN MIND Other great spots for a twirl on the ice are the Lasker and Wollman Memorial rinks (*see* Central Park), the latter offering a magical experience beneath the city skyline; Sky Rink (*see* Chelsea Piers); the World's Fair Ice Skating Rink (New York City Building south wing, Flushing Meadow Corona Park, Queens, tel. 718/271–1996); the Staten Island Skating Pavilion (30–80 Arthur Kill Rd., Staten Island, tel. 718/948–4800); and Brooklyn's Kate Wollman Center and Rink (*see* Prospect Park), not to be confused with Central Park's similarly named facility. Contact each for prices, hours, and seasons.

Bordered by 47th and 52nd Sts. and 5th and 7th Aves.; ice rink, between 49th and 50th Sts. and 5th and 6th Aves.

 Oct–Apr, M–Th 9 AM–10:30 PM, F–Sa 8:30–12, Su 8:30–10, (Nov–Jan, daily 8:30–12)

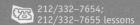 212/332–7654; 212/332–7655 lessons

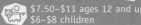 $7.50–$11 ages 12 and up, $6–$8 children

 2 and up

surrounded by flower beds filled with seasonal plantings in a setting conceived by artists, floral designers, and sculptors who present 10 shows each year. Somehow it manages to look great in any season. Below on the Lower Plaza, locate the famous gold-leaf statue of Prometheus, towering heroically over the ledge. The entrance of the 70-story GE Building (30 Rockefeller Plaza), once known as the RCA Building but now referred to as "30 Rock," is also guarded by another striking statue of Prometheus. It all makes Rockefeller Center a landmark of epic proportions.

KID-FRIENDLY EATS Dine by the rink at the **American Festival Cafe** (20 W. 50th St., tel. 212/332–7620). Holiday Skaters' Specials include skating, skate rental, and a meal. Or try the **Harley-Davidson Cafe** (1370 6th Ave., tel. 212/245–6000), **Television City** (70 W. 50th St., tel. 212/333–3388), or **Comedy Nation** (1626 Broadway, tel. 212/757–4100).

HEY, KIDS! The GE Building houses NBC headquarters (see NBC Studios Backstage Tour), and some of the first television programs originated from here. Nowadays *Today* broadcasts from a ground-floor glass-enclosed studio at 49th Street and Rockefeller Plaza. Be here between 7 and 9 AM to try to join the backdrop of faces behind the show's hosts. Bring a colorful sign saying hello to a loved one or proclaiming your hometown (if you're from out of town). You might get on TV!

RYE PLAYLAND

Go for the rides. Go for the fun. Go to sun, swim, play, or walk around, but go to Rye Playland.

This National Historic Landmark, opened in 1928, contains 45 rides today, including a log flume, haunted house, and separate Kiddyland just for the toddler set. (You'll even find pony rides here.) The carousel, built in 1915, is still going strong, and the trademark 82-foot Dragon Coaster is one of the last remaining historic wooden coasters in North America. Don't miss the spine-tingling Hurricane Roller Coaster and the Mind Scrambler—well, perhaps parents would just as soon miss this sensory experience. Also at the park are arcade games, the usual midway games, a lake with boat rides, a miniature golf course by the ocean, a saltwater beach, a boardwalk to amble on, and an Olympic-size pool.

To plan your day, start at the beach or pool, before the sun gets too hot, and lunch and munch on the boardwalk. By afternoon, it's off to the rides, along with a round of minigolf

TRANS-PORTA-TION The park is less than a 45-minute drive from the city. Take I–95 (the New England Thruway), and get off at Exit 19. Follow the signs to Play-land Parkway. Or call Westch-ester County Bee-line Buses (tel. 914/682–2020) for schedules.

KEEP IN MIND Remember to bring all the essentials: swimsuits, towels, beach toys, sunscreen, and water bottles—especially for your younger thrill seekers. Unlike the rest of this beautifully landscaped park, Kiddyland has no natural shade (or cool breezes). Bring blankets or lawn or beach chairs if you're staying for a concert. And of course, bring money. You can purchase individual tickets or ticket books, providing a reduced rate. Look for $2–$3 discount coupons in local magazines and newspapers, and if you find one, don't leave it at home.

and a boat ride. Avoid summer Tuesdays, when camp groups converge here. Be warned that Kiddyland gets crowded by midday, so you'll want to adjust your schedule to visit early or at dinner time. By early evening you'll be ready for a concert—usually musical nostalgia—which are staged often during July and August. Parents can bop to songs of the '50s, '60s, and '70s performed by many of the original artists, and kids can wonder why their parents are so weird.

Maintained by the Westchester County Parks Department, this old-fashioned amusement park is a beautiful setting dotted with Art Deco buildings straight out of the 1920s, meticulously groomed flower beds, and grassy, shady malls for strolling. It's a delight!

KID-FRIENDLY EATS It's hard to imagine coming here without letting your children sip slushies or get sticky with cotton candy for a snack break. There are sit-down tables and fast food galore throughout Playland, or you can pack a lunch and use the picnic tables. The foot-long Kosher hot dogs and fried dough are hard to resist. Cruise the boardwalk for additional fast-food fare.

SCHOMBURG CENTER

The Schomburg Center for Research in Black Culture, one of the research libraries of the New York Public Library system, is considered one of the leading institutions of its kind in the world. Devoted to the preservation of materials on black life, it is the guardian of over 5 million items, including over 3.5 million manuscript items, 125,000 books, and 300,000 photographs. Collections of magazines, posters, art objects, films, videotapes, audio recordings, and memorabilia are also included.

Tours, exhibitions, forums, film screenings, and performing arts bring black history and culture to life for both young and old. Thanks to a 350-seat state-of-the-art auditorium, a 75-seat theater/auditorium, and a 30-seat screening room, the Schomburg Center sponsors over 60 programs each year, including poetry readings, plays, concerts, lectures, and panel discussions. Regular exhibitions are mounted in the gallery and exhibition hall. The Art and Artifacts collection holds over 20,000 items in three areas: paintings and sculpture, works on paper, and textiles and artifacts. It is particularly strong in art produced during the Harlem

KEEP IN MIND Other Harlem sights include the Abyssinian Baptist Church (132 Odell Clark Pl. W, tel. 212/862–7474), pulpit for two famous Adam Clayton Powells, one of whom was also a congressman. Tour the Apollo Theatre (253 W. 125th St., tel. 212/749–5838). The Studio Museum in Harlem (144 W. 125th St., tel. 212/864–4500), a small art museum, has a sculpture garden and a collection of paintings and photographs. Off the beaten path but worthwhile is the American Numismatic Society (Broadway at 155th St., tel. 212/234–3130) and its coins and medals.

 515 Malcolm X Blvd.

 212/491-2200

 Free

M–Sa 10–6, Su 1–5

 9 and up

Renaissance. Portraits of many famous 19th- and 20th-century black artists, politicians, actors, musicians, athletes, and social activists are included.

Take time to look at the New York Black 100 Project, an exhibition of the 100 most significant black New Yorkers of the 20th century, chosen from among public nominations. The resulting exhibition is as powerful as the list of names, an impressive who's who of athletes, politicians, musicians, entertainers, activists, artists, authors, and personalities. Langston Hughes, Malcolm X, Jackie Robinson, Alvin Ailey, Maya Angelou, Matthew Henson (explorer), and Gordon Parks (photographer) are all here. See how many you and your children recognize, and discuss the contributions that each one made to society. If your knowledge is lacking, there is no better place to learn about the influence of black Americans on our history and culture than the Schomburg Center.

KID-FRIENDLY EATS Catercorner from the Schomburg Center stands the **Pan Pan Restaurant** (500 Lenox Ave., tel. 212/926–4900). Go for grits, fried chicken, delicious desserts, or a bite any time. For southern specialties and home-style cooking, friendly service, and perhaps a chat with owner-hostess Sylvia Woods, head to **Sylvia's** (328 Lenox Ave., tel. 212/996–0660).

HEY, KIDS! Inlaid in the floor of the airy lobby of the Langston Hughes Auditorium is *Rivers*, an artistic work that's a tribute to Hughes (1902–1967), writer of plays, stories, books, newspaper sketches, and, most notably, poems. If you haven't read anything by him, read his poem "A Dream Deferred." He penned many of his Jesse B. Semple or "Simple" columns about Harlem life in a brownstone at 20 East 127th Street, between Madison and 5th avenues (open by appointment only, tel. 212/534–5992).

SONY IMAX THEATRE

This theater, located at Lincoln Square's Sony Theatres, offers a sight and sound experience the likes of which you and your children probably have never experienced.

The screen, which measures 100 feet wide and 80 feet high—the same height as an eight-story building—is the largest in the Western Hemisphere. A six-channel digital sound system has loudspeakers controlled by 18,000 watts of power distributed around the front and rear of the facility, surrounding you in sound. And taking IMAX—the world's largest film format—one step further, films shown here are 3-D. No wonder that since its opening in 1994 the theater has ranked among the highest-grossing single movie screens in the United States.

Steep rows of stadium seats offer good views from anywhere in the theater. You are given lightweight 3-D headsets with liquid-crystal lenses. The cordless shuttered lenses receive infrared signals from the projector, causing each lens to alternately and rapidly open and

KID-FRIENDLY EATS Have a bit of fish-and-chips at **Mad Fish** (2182 Broadway, tel. 212/787–0202). For some comfort food in large portions, visit the **Brooklyn Diner USA** (212 W. 57th St., tel. 212/581–8900).

KEEP IN MIND The experience here may be overwhelming for some youngsters, even at the upper elementary school ages. To help you determine whether current or coming attractions are appropriate and for more information on the theater, visit Sony's Web site at www.sony.com (go to "Pictures"). Carefully survey the offerings for subject matter. A child afraid of heights, for example, would not fare well watching *Everest*. Some films are scary, made more so by the 3-D. Those with a lot of aerial shots might make youngsters (and others) dizzy, perhaps even queasy. Some are loud!

close, creating the perception of one three-dimensional image. But you don't have to dwell on how it works. Just see it to believe it.

Breathtaking films like *Everest* take you to the summit of the world's tallest and most challenging mountain. *NY 3D: Across the Sea of Time* lets you travel to New York City with a young immigrant boy to experience the city with the innocent and appreciative eyes of a visitor from another land. The unparalleled realism of *T-REX: Back to the Cretaceous* gives you the thrill of bringing the dinosaurs back to life. Films change periodically, but rest assured: The new crop will be just as grand, inspiring, thrilling, and impressive.

HEY, KIDS! You may have had a 3-D experience before, but it probably wasn't like this one! After you see a movie here, compare the special effects to other 3-D events you've experienced. Or ask your parents or grandparents to describe their memories of 3-D movies. Technology has changed significantly since the '50s and the days of those green and red 3-D glasses that were distributed to moviegoers and comic book fans.

SONY WONDER TECHNOLOGY LAB

From the moment you are greeted outside the Sony Wonder Technology Lab by b.b. wonderbot, the interactive robot, you feel the excitement of cutting-edge communication technology. Enter your name, have your picture taken, and record your voice at the sign-in station, located at the twinkling fiber-optic lights, to obtain your personalized "swipe cards," which allow access to 38 exciting and inviting interactive exhibits.

Don't be surprised if you see your picture or hear your voice pop up throughout your visit. You're not just going to see technology; you will become part of it during an adventure through four floors of hands-on educational fun. Don't despair if you and your kids are not techno-whizzes; helpful guides throughout the lab will answer your questions and offer assistance.

Okay. Roll 'em, as your children take part in a production in the television studio or join the crew inside a digital recording studio to learn to mix a song with a Sony artist. They can

HEY, KIDS! He's a mess of wires, microchips, and a whole lot of attitude. He's b.b. wonderbot, the lab's robot star and official greeter. Wonder how he can answer all the questions he's asked? Telepresence technology (a.k.a. remote control) enables a human operator to work him from inside the building. With miniature cameras hidden in b.b.'s eyeballs and microphones in his head, the operator can see and hear people nearby and can direct the robot's remarkably lifelike movement as well as take part in conversations.

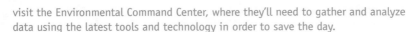
visit the Environmental Command Center, where they'll need to gather and analyze data using the latest tools and technology in order to save the day.

If your children want to surf the Web, they can do that from various computer stations, but they might want to save this for home or the library, so they can do the things they can only do here. Take a break in the 72-seat High Definition Theater, where you can sample the latest in High Definition Television, coming soon to a TV near you.

For a historical perspective, the Communications Bridge covers 150 years in the history and development of technology. Look for red circles along the way, which highlight important inventions. And just think: One day, all these exciting new technologies will just be red circles in some future historical display.

KID-FRIENDLY EATS The **Berkeley Bar and Grill** (tel. 212/833–7800), in Sony Plaza, serves lunch for families on the go. A takeout kiosk run by the restaurant offers bagels, sandwiches, and soups for those even more on the go, or who want to picnic in the plaza. **Mangia** (16 E. 48th St., tel. 212/754–7600) has tempting sandwiches, salad, and antipasto.

KEEP IN MIND This place is a true bargain. Admission to this nifty wonderland of technology is free, as are screenings of popular movies shown evenings in the High Definition Theater. Even the children's workshops, scheduled on select Saturdays and Sundays, cost only a moderate fee. Students in grades 1–12 can take part in innovative and creative sessions in which they can learn the science of animation, create their own video short, produce a family video documentary, or dissect the similarities between the human eye and the camera.

SOUTH STREET SEAPORT MUSEUM

Nestled within an 11-block historic district of restored 18th- and 19th-century buildings and sailing ships, this museum actually comprises a number of facilities: a visitor center, Children's Center, Maritime Crafts Center, library, three galleries, a fleet of sailing ships, and re-created printing shop as well as the off-site New York Unearthed (*see above*). But they're all dedicated to chronicling the history of New York's original seaport and its commercial and cultural impact on the city, the state, and the nation.

Set sail for another place and time with a map and schedule from the visitor center. Whether it's a concert, a show by street performers, guided tours, or family programs, there is always something happening at the museum. Family Gallery Guides direct you around the world's largest collection of objects related to New York's port. Over 2 million archaeological artifacts, fine and decorative folk arts, ship models, scrimshaw, and maps are showcased in the Whitman, Melville, and Norway galleries.

HEY, KIDS!

If a visit here tickled your sails, why not come back for more? Learn to furl a sail, tie a knot, or chart a course at a three-hour sailor certificate program. In the Afterschool Arts Crew, children 8–12 explore port history through varied activities once a week for seven weeks.

KEEP IN MIND
Among the district's sights, the Titanic Memorial (Fulton and Water Sts.) is a small lighthouse commemorating the 1912 sinking. Follow Fulton Street's cobblestones to Schermerhorn Row, a redbrick terrace of Georgian and Federal warehouses and countinghouses housing shops and restaurants. Take an *early* (3–8 AM) stroll through the Fulton Fish Market, the nation's largest and oldest (since the 1770s) wholesale fish market. During warm months, the museum runs tours.

Visitor center, 12 Fulton St.; Children's Center, 165 John St.; Whitman and Melville galleries, Water St.; Norway Galleries, John St.

Apr–Sept, Th 10–8, F–W 10–6; Oct–Mar, W–M 10–5

 212/748–8600

 $6 ages 13 and up, $3 children 12 and under

 3 and up

Three historic museum vessels are open for tours, including the *Peking* and the *Wavertree* (large sailing cargo ships) and a lightship, the *Ambrose*. Explore the harbor on the *W.O. Decker*, a 1930 tugboat that worked this waterfront. Or climb aboard the *Pioneer*, a historic schooner, for a fun-filled ride. Sailing instruction for teens is offered on the *Lettie G. Howard*, a fully restored 1893 fishing schooner, now a National Historic Landmark.

Your family can visit the Maritime Crafts Center, where model-builders and a wood-carver ply their trades. At Bowne & Company Stationers, a re-creation of a 19th-century printing shop, artisans demonstrate the skills that made the city the nation's printing capital. The museum's Children's Center offers interactive exhibits, family programs, and educational games that make history come alive for children. On weekends, holidays, and school vacations, crafts workshops related to museum themes and exhibits are held. Performers and storytellers are also featured periodically.

KID-FRIENDLY EATS Grab a burger, hot dog, pizza, or salad at the **Promenade Food Court** (Pier 17, 3rd floor). Don't miss the view from the tables in the glass-walled atrium. For hearty, sumptuous soup try **Seaport Soup Company** (76 Fulton St., tel. 212/693–1371). You can also get it to go. If your kind of town is Chicago and your kind of pizza is deep dish, head to **Pizzeria Uno Chicago** (89 South St., Pier 17, tel. 212/791–7999) and pile the toppings high.

STATEN ISLAND CHILDREN'S MUSEUM

How would your children like to crawl through an ant home, watch a butterfly being born, or listen to an insect chorus? They can do that and more at the Staten Island Children's Museum. Located in an 82-acre park, the museum occupies 10,000 square feet of a four-story building boasting an Italianate facade. An imposing porpoise, hanging in the central atrium, greets you. Exhibits tackle subjects from many different perspectives, incorporating the arts, science, and the humanities with an inviting child-friendly approach.

The Bugs and Other Insects exhibit invites big and not-so-big people into the miniature world of insects. If insects bug your kids, a quick trip to Block Harbor will put them back on an even keel. This waterfront setting, complete with pirate ship and gangplank, is an imaginative play space containing blocks and a menagerie of animal toys. Kids jump right in to the Wonder Water exhibit, which highlights the unique properties of that vital part of our world. A collection of tubs and sinks, boats, water wheels, terrariums and aquariums, and a babbling brook beckon.

KEEP IN MIND You can become family members of both the Staten Island Zoo and Staten Island Children's Museum for $80. Membership benefits include admission to both, as well as admission to more than 100 reciprocating zoos in the United States and Canada; advance notice of special events; sneak previews for new exhibits; invitations to "members only" events; discounts on gift shop purchases, museum birthday parties, special programs, and summer minicamps; special offers from local businesses; the zoo magazine and calendar; and the museum newsletter.

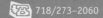 Snug Harbor Cultural Center, 1000 Richmond Terr., Staten Island

 $4 ages 2 and up

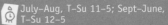 July–Aug, T–Su 11–5; Sept–June, T–Su 12–5

718/273–2060

 2 and up

Meet you in the Animal Diner, part of the Animals Eat: Different Feasts for Different Beasts exhibit. Here children can find out what the live animals are having for dinner and learn about the food chain. Portia's Playhouse is an interactive theater space where kids try on masks or costumes and use props, puppets, sound effects, lights, and other theater equipment in imaginative play. The Walk-In! Workshop is a classroom activity center equipped with self-directed art activities and materials.

First founded in 1974 by a group of parents from the community, the Staten Island Children's Museum moved to its current site in 1986. Museum interpreters are always on hand to animate and explain exhibit themes and activities. School and community programs, traveling exhibitions, family workshops, hands-on science activities, and performances spotlighting storytelling, dance, drama, and puppetry are all part of the fun and learning at the museum.

KID-FRIENDLY EATS **Goodfella's Brick Oven Pizza** (1718 Hylan Blvd., tel. 718/987–2422) will make you an offer you can't refuse: great pizza. Try the killer chili at **Adobe Blues Restaurant** (63 Lafayette St., tel. 718/720–2583), a southwestern-style eating place just off Richmond Terrace.

HEY, KIDS! There are so many different ways to "do" this museum. Want to watch the stars come out here? The museum sponsors sleep overs. Feel like celebrating? You can have a birthday party here, perhaps based on a museum exhibit, or a cooking, a chocolate, or an ice cream party, too. During school holiday recesses, the museum offers many exciting programs, free with admission, whereas "make and take" craft sessions carry a materials fee.

STATEN ISLAND ZOO

How many legs does an African millipede have? How far can a snowy owl turn its head? How big is a baby King Island wallaby when it's born? For the answers to these and other animal queries, visit the Staten Island Zoo. On 8 acres in a manicured park setting, New York City's biggest little zoo features an African savanna, aquarium, and tropical forest.

The African Savannah exhibit re-creates this ecosystem at twilight and features meerkats, a burrowing python, leopards, bush babies, and rock hyrax—curious creatures that look like rodents but are actually most closely related to elephants. The Tropical Forest exhibit highlights the endangered South American rain forest and the animals that dwell within. Here your family can watch the piranha, spider monkeys, ocelots, short-tailed leaf-nosed fruit bats, and iguanas in a natural flow of flora and fauna.

HEY, KIDS!
Snakes Alive! If you love things that slink and slither, check out the Carl Kaufeld Serpentarium, which features an internationally acclaimed display of reptiles. In fact, it has one of the most extensive collections of North American rattlesnakes anywhere.

The wraparound aquarium exhibit spotlights marine life from all over the world, whereas the Children's Center resembles a New England farm, complete with a covered bridge

KEEP IN MIND Plan your day at the zoo so you don't miss the action during feeding times. The reptiles chow down at 2:30 PM on Sunday. The sharks and piranha at the aquarium break for a bite at 1 on Thursday. (Don't worry. They do eat more than once a week; they just don't eat in front of an audience at other times.) Join the bats from 2 to 3 every day for a meal in the Tropical Forest.

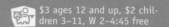

overlooking a duck pond. Here your children can meet an interesting array of international domestic farm animals. Be sure to visit the Pony Barn and Track.

Special programs are held throughout the year with some—like Maple Sugaring, Puppet Shows, and Worm Weather Gear—requiring preregistration and a nominal fee. Other events—like Leapin' Lizards, Fine Feathered Faces, Hats Off to Giraffes, Eat Like a Bird, and Children Against Litterbugs—are free. Many programs are offered in conjunction with the Staten Island Children's Museum.

The zoo is a great place to celebrate Groundhog Day. Chuck, New York City's only weather-predicting groundhog, greets visitors throughout the day after a 7:30 AM prediction proclamation. Hardy souls who brave the cold to cheer the resident rodent share coffee, juice, bagels, and the fun of witnessing Chuck's moment in the sun (or shadow).

KID-FRIENDLY EATS Visit the **snack bar** (tel. 718/720–7218) for a convenient lunch or midday snack. Or try the neighborhood **Elm Park Inn** (238 Morning Star Rd., tel. 718/720–1983), between Forest Avenue and Richmond Terrace, for oversize portions and family dining. No weekend reservations are taken here, so expect a wait.

STATUE OF LIBERTY

"Give me your tired, your poor, / Your huddled masses yearning to breathe free. . . ." Many people recognize the opening lines of the poem "The New Colossus," which is inscribed on the Statue of Liberty. Everyone recognizes the sentiment. For over 100 years, this historic monument has served as a universal beacon of hope and opportunity, a symbol of freedom, and a gift of international friendship. It is one of our nation's most heavily visited attractions, popular with both kids and adults. The official name of the statue is Liberty Enlightening the World, and for over a century, she has done as her inscription reads: "I lift my lamp beside the golden door."

The statue was sculpted by August Bartholdi, who first traveled to America in 1871 to propose the monument and choose a suitable site. Built in 1884 in France, the statue stood in Paris until it was dismantled and sent to the United States in 1885. A foundation and pedestal were created here, and the completed monument was dedicated on October 28, 1886. By the 1980s, a complete refurbishment was needed, and a team of French and American artisans

HEY, KIDS! Ready for the climb to the crown? You have two options. You can take an elevator 10 stories to the top of the pedestal, where there's an awesome view of Manhattan, and then climb 168 steps to the crown. Or, if you're really ready for a challenge, you can climb the whole thing—364 steps (the equivalent of 22 stories) from bottom to top. You're not allowed to go up into the torch, though. Sorry!

worked for two years repairing and replacing as necessary to keep the sculptor's original creation shining in the harbor. In 1986, the fruits of their labor were harvested, as the statue celebrated her centennial.

One of the main reasons to visit the statue, of course, is to climb to the crown. But even those who venture no further than the pedestal will have much to see and do. A museum here features exhibits detailing how the statue was built, and the promenade, colonnade, and top level of the pedestal offer spectacular views of New York Harbor. Videos of the view from the crown are shown for those unable or unwilling to make the climb to the top, and life-size castings of the face and foot of the statue are available for sight-impaired visitors to feel. As she always has, Lady Liberty welcomes all.

KID-FRIENDLY EATS There's a pleasant outdoor **café** on Liberty Island. You can also pack a picnic to eat along the way, or after your return on the ferry, go to one of the eateries mentioned in Ellis Island, Fraunces Tavern Museum, New York Unearthed, and South Street Seaport Museum.

KEEP IN MIND In summer, it's not uncommon to wait two–four hours to climb to the crown, for either option. There's no shade, and waiting can be hard on kids; bring water bottles, juice boxes, and small toys to amuse them. Saturdays are less crowded than Sundays. It's a good idea to ask how long the wait for the crown is before buying tickets. The ticket office for both the Statue of Liberty and Ellis Island is at Castle Clinton National Monument (*see above*), a restored brick fortress in Manhattan's Battery Park.

THEODORE ROOSEVELT BIRTHPLACE

3

Though the building here isn't the real brownstone where Teddy Roosevelt was born—it's a 1923 reconstruction—it does teach a lot about the real life of the nation's 26th president. Five period rooms—the library, dining room, parlor (the most elegant room in the house), master bedroom, and nursery—are furnished with many items from the original house, pieces belonging to other family members, and other decorative period pieces. Two obelisks in the library are souvenirs of a family trip to Egypt. The horsehair chair seats in the dining room are said to have scratched Roosevelt's legs during his early childhood. In addition, two museum galleries display a variety of historical items, including journals, family photographs, political buttons and cartoons, articles of clothing including Roosevelt's Rough Rider uniform, and his crib.

The site offers a window on what mid-19th-century life was like for a wealthy family living on a once-quiet, tree-lined street in a most fashionable New York City neighborhood. Memorabilia reveals much about the man who would become not only president of the United

KEEP IN MIND For those interested in following TR through his later years, visit the Sagamore Hill National Historic Site (Cove Neck Rd., Oyster Bay, tel. 516/922–4788), on Long Island. Roosevelt's home for most of his adult life, it contains original furnishings and memorabilia.

HEY, KIDS! Do you have a favorite teddy bear? The teddy bear was actually named for Teddy Roosevelt, who once refused to shoot a captive bear on a hunting trip. Political cartoonists poked fun of the incident, but a Brooklyn toy maker asked Roosevelt's permission to make stuffed bears and call them "Teddy's bears." The upper museum room has one of these original bears along with cartoons, books, writing paper, ceramic figures, and other objects with teddy bear images. Does your bear look like one of "Teddy's bears?"

States but also vice president, governor of New York, assistant secretary of the Navy, police commissioner, New York State assemblyman, and Rough Rider, as well as a rancher and cowboy.

As a young child, Theodore, called Teedie by his family, was a thin and sickly child who suffered from severe asthma. His father made the bedroom behind his nursery into an open-air porch by taking out a wall and putting up a railing. He also installed gym equipment so Teedie could exercise and improve his health. Roosevelt and friends used to climb through the nursery windows to get to the outdoor porch and equipment. He obviously overcame his frailty.

The Life and Times of Theodore Roosevelt, a 30-minute documentary narrated by Walter Cronkite, highlights Roosevelt's life, including scenes of 19th-century New York City. *Teedie,* also a 30-minute film, tells the story of the young Teddy who lived here. Other biographical films are sometimes shown as well, and concerts, lectures, and special events are scheduled throughout the year.

KID-FRIENDLY EATS For an endless menu, substantial portions, and reasonable prices, try **America** (9 E. 18th St., tel. 212/505–2110). On weekends kids get crayons and coloring books, and a magician and balloon artist perform on Sunday.

TOP OF THE WORLD TRADE CENTER

Y ou can't top the Top of the World, the World Trade Center's "theme park in the sky," when it comes to seeing all of New York City in a day. The panoramic vista, 1,377 feet above sea level, offers a view of the city second to none. From the open-air observation deck on the 110th floor, you and your children can take in views of the city and land beyond that extend up to 55 miles in three states. You can also enjoy the scenery from the glass-enclosed observatory on the 107th floor. And whereas the daytime views from the top of the World Trade Center are spectacular, evening hours offer a city lights show not to be missed.

But let's start on the ground. The two skyscrapers that make up the World Trade Center sit on 16 acres, almost the size of 16 football fields. This city within a city is the daily workplace for 50,000 people, and over 200,000 people visit the Twin Towers each day.

The observatories can be reached from the mezzanine level of the lobby by taking either of two express elevators that travel 107 floors in less than a minute. Once up top, take a self-

KEEP IN MIND While you're at the top, try to locate famous landmarks: St. Paul's Chapel (1776), the city's oldest public building, at Broadway and Fulton Street; the Brooklyn Bridge, completed in 1883; the 1901 Flatiron Building, the city's oldest remaining skyscraper; the Woolworth Building (1913); the Chrysler Building, with its stainless-steel needle and Art Deco style; the Empire State Building, previously the city's tallest building; South Street Seaport; Kennedy Airport; Washington Arch, in Greenwich Village's Washington Square Park; Battery Park; the Statue of Liberty; and Ellis Island.

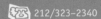

guided tour of the city through any of the 44 multilingual skyline viewers. Next, see how many landmarks you can spot in the 750-building model of Manhattan, and don't forget to study the wall murals that depict city neighborhoods.

You literally have the Big Apple at your feet when you experience the 3-D floor map and digital display walls that spotlight all the sights below. Fasten your seat belt before taking a free simulated helicopter ride through the streets. A kinetic-energy wall sculpture is a captivating display, especially for young ones. Another fascinating stop is New York's Schools in the Sky, where digital transmitting stations allow youngsters to create "messages to the stars" by sending their names and personalized messages into space through a beam of light. Gift shops offer something for everyone.

KID-FRIENDLY EATS The **Sbarro Street Station food court,** modeled after the subway, has sandwiches, pizza, salads, sweets, and **Nathan's Famous** hot dogs. The seating area looks like Central Park. If your local golden arches doesn't sport a doorman and pianist, visit this **McDonald's** (160 Broadway, tel. 212/385-2063), with a stock ticker above the counter.

HEY, KIDS! Since the World Trade Center opened in 1975, 30 million people have zoomed up those express elevators to the top. But a few people skipped the traditional ride for a more scenic route. In 1974, Philippe Petit walked a tightrope from the corner of Tower 2 to the roof of Tower 1. In 1977, George Willig used suction cups to inch his way up the northeast wall to the top. Don't try this at home—or at the World Trade Center, for that matter!

UNITED NATIONS

If you come on a working day, you'll see all 185 U.N. members' flags flying above 1st Avenue—from Afghanistan to Zimbabwe. It's an impressive sight, but so is the rest of U.N. Headquarters and the United Nations itself. Created in 1945, it joins countries working for world peace and against poverty and injustice.

As you enter headquarters gates, you're stepping into an "international zone," belonging not just to the United States but to all member nations. It has its own fire and security forces and its own post office, where you can post only mail bearing U.N. stamps. Mail a postcard to yourself as a souvenir.

One-hour guided tours include an explanation of the aims, structure, and activities of the organization as well as descriptions of art and architecture featured en route. Tours are given in many languages. What else would you expect at an institution with six official languages: Arabic, Chinese, English, French, Russian, and Spanish?

HEY, KIDS! You've heard of the Magic School Bus? Now you can ride on the CyberSchool bus (www.un.org/Pubs/CyberSchoolBus). This Web site offers a wealth of information, activities, and resources about the United Nations and worldwide concerns. Plan to "take a ride" before or after your visit. There are on-line puzzles and games for all ages. Try the Flag Tag or the Doctor's Data Quiz. Check out InfoNation, an interactive database that lets you compare information about several countries at a time. (Great for schoolwork!)

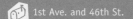
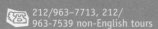
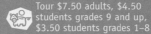
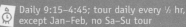

On most days, tours take in many of these areas: General Assembly, Security Council Chamber, Trustee Council Chambers, Economic and Social Council Chamber, Rose Garden, lobby, and public concourse. In the lobby, noteworthy gifts to the U.N. include a model of Sputnik I from the Soviet Union, moon rock from the United States, a statue of Poseidon from Greece, and a 15-foot by 30-foot stained-glass Chagall window presented by the artist in memory of Secretary General Dag Hammarskjold. Other artworks include the mosaic *Dove of Peace,* presented by Pope John Paul II, in the General Assembly lobby; *Non-violence,* a bronze replica of a revolver tied in a knot, from Luxembourg, by the General Assembly building; and a Norman Rockwell mosaic, near the Economic and Social Council Chamber, inscribed, "Do unto others as you would have them do unto you." In truth, your children might practice the golden rule better than some U.N. members, but amazingly, after over 50 years, this organization still strives to unite very disparate nations.

KID-FRIENDLY EATS The **Coffee Shop,** located at the U.N.'s public concourse, is open daily—first-come, first-served. For big portions of all the foods Mom used to make, try the **Comfort Diner** (214 E. 45th St., tel. 212/867-4555).

KEEP IN MIND Surfing isn't just for kids. At the U.N. home page (www.un.org), you can take an on-line tour before your visit; get up-to-date information about U.N. work in areas like peace and security, economic and social development, and human rights; and browse press releases and daily highlights, often before printed versions are released. You can also get free publications (in several languages) from the U.N. and many of its agencies and programs.

games

THE CLASSICS

"I'M THINKING OF AN ANIMAL..." With older kids you can play 20 Questions: Have your leader think of an animal, vegetable, or mineral (or, alternatively, a person, place, or thing) and let everybody else try to guess what it is. The correct guesser takes over as leader. If no one figures out the secret within 20 questions, the first person goes again. With younger children, limit the guessing to animals and don't put a ceiling on how many questions can be asked. With rivalrous siblings, just take turns being leader. Make the game's theme things you expect to see at your day's destination.

"I SEE SOMETHING YOU DON'T SEE AND IT IS BLUE."
Stuck for a way to get your youngsters to settle down in a museum? Sit them down on a bench in the middle of a room and play this vintage favorite. The leader gives just one clue—the color—and everybody guesses away.

FUN WITH THE ALPHABET

"I'M GOING TO THE GROCERY..." The first player begins, "I'm going to the grocery and I'm going to buy... " and finishes the sentence with the name of an object, found in grocery stores, that begins with the letter "A". The second player repeats what the first player has said, and adds the name of another item that starts with "B". The third player repeats everything that has been said so far and adds something that begins with "C" and so on through the alphabet. Anyone who skips or misremembers an item is out (or decide up front that you'll give hints to all who need 'em). You can modify the theme depending on where you're going that day, as "I'm going to X and I'm going to see..."

"I'M GOING TO ASIA ON AN ANT TO ACT UP." Working their way through the alphabet, players concoct silly sentences stating where they're going, how they're traveling, and what they'll do.

FAMILY ARK Noah had his ark—here's your chance to build your own. It's easy: Just start naming animals and work your way through the alphabet, from antelope to zebra.

WHAT I SEE, FROM A TO Z In this game, kids look for objects in alphabetical order—first something whose name begins with "A", next an item whose name begins with "B", and so on. If you're in the car, have children do their spotting through their own window. Whoever gets to Z first wins. Or have each child play to beat his own time. Try this one as you make your way through zoos and museums, too.

JUMP-START A CONVERSATION

WHAT IF...? Riding in the car and waiting in a restaurant are great times to get to know your youngsters better. Begin with imaginative questions to prime the pump.

• If you were the tallest man on earth, what would your life be like? The shortest?
• If you had a magic carpet, where would you go? Why? What would you do there?
• If your parents gave you three wishes, what would they be?
• If you were elected president, what changes would you make?
• What animal would you like to be and what would your life be like?
• What's a friend? Who are your best friends? What do you like to do together?
• Describe a day in your life 10 years from now.

DRUTHERS How do your kids really feel about things? Just ask. "Would you rather eat worms or hamburgers? Hamburgers or candy?" Choose serious and silly topics—and have fun!

FAKER, FAKER Reveal three facts about yourself. The catch: One of the facts is a fake. Have your kids ferret out the fiction. Take turns being the faker. Fakers who stump everyone win.

KEEP A STRAIGHT FACE

"HA!" Work your way around the car. First person says "Ha." Second person says "Ha, ha." Third person says "Ha" three times. And so on. Just try to keep a straight face. Or substitute "Here, kitty, kitty, kitty!"

WIGGLE & GIGGLE Give your kids a chance to stick out their tongues at you. Start by making a face, then have the next person imitate you and add a gesture of his own—snapping fingers, winking, clapping, sneezing, or the like. The next person mimics the first two and adds a third gesture, and so on.

JUNIOR OPERA During a designated period of time, have your kids sing everything they want to say.

IGPAY ATINLAY Proclaim the next 30 minutes Pig Latin time, and everybody has to talk in this fun code. To speak it, move the first consonant of every word to the end of the word and add "ay." "Pig" becomes "igpay," and "Latin" becomes "atinlay." To words that being with a vowel, just add "ay" as a suffix.

MORE GOOD TIMES

BUILD A STORY   "Once upon a time there lived…" Finish the sentence and ask the rest of your family, one at a time, to add another sentence or two. Bring a tape recorder along to record the narrative—and you can enjoy your creation again and again.

NOT THE GOOFY GAME   Have one child name a category. (Some ideas: first names, last names, animals, countries, friends, feelings, foods, hot or cold things, clothing.) Then take turns naming things that fall into that category. You're out if you name something that doesn't belong in the category—or if you can't think of another item to name. When only one person remains, start again. Choose categories depending on where you're going or where you've been—historic topics if you've seen a historic sight, animal topics before or after the zoo, upside-down things if you've been to the circus, and so on. Make the game harder by choosing category items in A-B-C order.

COLOR OF THE DAY Choose a color at the beginning of your outing and have your kids be on the lookout for things that are that color, calling out what they've seen when they spot it. If you want to keep score, keep a running list or use a pen to mark points on your kids' hands for every item they spot.

CLICK If Cam Jansen, the heroine of a popular series of early-reader books, says "Click" as she looks at something, she can remember every detail of what she sees, like a camera (that's how she got her nickname). Say "Click!" Then give each one of your kids a full minute to study a page of a magazine. After everyone has had a turn, go around the car naming items from the page. Players who can't name an item or who make a mistake are out.

THE QUIET GAME Need a good giggle—or a moment of calm to figure out your route? The driver sets a time limit and everybody must be silent. The last person to make a sound wins.

THEMATIC INDEX

FARMS & ANIMALS

FOOD FIXATION

FREEBIES

PERFORMANCES

PLANES, TRAINS, AND AUTOMOBILES

RAINY DAYS

ACKNOWLEDGMENTS

In the 70s, my boyfriend—now husband—and I would joke that we were off on another "family adventure" as we explored parks, museums, and other attractions. No family, of course. Today, almost a quarter century later, we still take those family adventures, but now with three children in tow. As a parent, a teacher, and writer, I look for those "teachable moments" to share with my children. I must confess that with a 4 year-old, an 11 year-old, and a 13 year-old, it is often challenging to find something of interest for everyone, parents included. This edition was written with that in mind.

Many thanks to the public relations professionals at each of our sights who were so helpful in answering questions and checking facts (and opinions). This book is lovingly dedicated to Rachel ("Are we there yet?"); Jennifer ("Can we listen to the car radio instead of those baby tapes?"); and Michael ("When are we leaving?").

—Mindy Bailin